IN
PRAISE
OF
Sailors

I will go back to the great sweet mother, —
    Mother and lover of men, the Sea.
I will go down to her, I and none other,
    Close with her, kiss her, and mix her with me;
Cling to her, strive with her, hold her fast;
    O fair white mother, in days long past
Born without sister, born without brother,
    Set free my soul as thy soul is free.

HOWARD PYLE / ALGERNON CHARLES SWINBURNE

A NAUTICAL ANTHOLOGY OF  ART, POETRY, AND PROSE

IN PRAISE OF
Sailors

COMPILED AND EDITED BY

Herbert W. Warden, III

HARRY N. ABRAMS, INC. / PUBLISHERS, NEW YORK

PROJECT MANAGER: *Robert Morton*
EDITOR: *Margaret Donovan*
DESIGNER: *Jos. Trautwein*

"Names Are Ships" and "How to Know Hawaii" from *Vagabond's House* by Don Blanding. Copyright 1928, 1956 by Don Blanding. Reprinted by permission of Dodd, Mead & Company, Inc.

"Flying Cloud" by Michael F. Blaser. Copyright 1977 by Michael F. Blaser and reproduced by his permission.

"After Forty Year" from *The Brassbounder* by David W. Bone. Copyright, 1921, by E. P. Dutton & Co.; renewal, 1949 by David W. Bone. Reprinted by permission of the publishers, E. P. Dutton and Gerald Duckworth & Co. Ltd.

"You and Us," from *The Ways of Many Waters* by Edwin James Brady. Reprinted by permission of Bulletin Newspaper Company, Sydney, Australia.

The etchings of Arthur Briscoe from *Arthur Briscoe-Marine Artist*. Reproduced by permission of Teredo Books Limited, Brighton, England, and Mr. Trevor-Briscoe.

The watercolors of Arthur Briscoe reproduced by permission of Mr. Trevor-Briscoe.

The Moonrakers by Robert Carse. Copyright © 1961 by Robert Carse. Reprinted by permission of Harper & Row, Publishers, Inc.

Joseph Conrad: Life and Letters by Jean-Aubry. Reprinted by permission of Doubleday & Company, Inc.

"Masts Against the Sky," "The Thermopylae Leaving Foochow," and "The Rising Wind" by Montague Dawson copyright Frost & Reed Limited.

"Burial At Sea," "The Gwydyr Castle," "Lee Braces," and "Running Before the Gale" by Anton Otto Fischer from *Anton Otto Fischer–Marine Artist*. Reproduced by permission of Teredo Books Limited, Brighton, England.

Focs'le Days by Anton Otto Fischer. Copyright 1947 by Charles Scribner's Sons, renewed 1975 by Katrina Sigsbee Fischer. Reprinted by permission of Katrina Sigsbee Fischer.

Library of Congress Cataloging in Publication Data

Main entry under title:
In praise of sailors.

   1. Seafaring life—Addresses, essays, lectures.
I. Warden, Herbert W., III
G540.I43   910'.45   78-6810
ISBN 0-8109-1107-8

Library of Congress Catalogue Card Number: 78-6810

Pen and ink drawings by Lyle Galloway. Copyright © 1978 by Lyle Galloway.

"Who Pilots Ships" from *Bright Harbor* by Daniel Whitehead Hicky. Copyright 1932, © 1960 by Daniel Whitehead Hicky. Reprinted by permission of Holt, Rinehart and Winston, Publishers.

Rudyard Kipling's Verse: Definitive Edition. Reprinted by permission of the Executors of the Estate of Mrs. George Bambridge, Doubleday & Company, Inc., The National Trust, Methuen & Son Ltd., and the Macmillan Co. of London & Basingstoke.

The Dream and Other Poems by John Masefield. Copyright 1922, 1923 by John Masefield, renewed 1950, 1951 by John Masefield. Reprinted with permission of Macmillan Publishing Co., Inc., and The Society of Authors as the literary representative of the Estate of John Masefield.

Poems by John Masefield. Reprinted with the permission of Macmillan Publishing Co., Inc., and The Society of Authors as the literary representative of the Estate of John Masefield.

The Story of a Round-House and Other Poems by John Masefield. Copyright 1912 by Macmillan Publishing Company, Inc., renewed 1940 by John Masefield. Reprinted with permission of Macmillan Publishing Co., Inc., and The Society of Authors as the literary representative of the Estate of John Masefield.

Tarpaulin Muster by John Masefield. Reprinted with the permission of The Society of Authors as the literary representative of the Estate of John Masefield.

The Wanderer of Liverpool by John Masefield. Copyright 1930 by John Masefield, renewed 1958 by John Masefield. Reprinted with permission of Macmillan Publishing Co., Inc., and The Society of Authors as the literary representative of the Estate of John Masefield.

Sailor Historian: The Best of Samuel Eliot Morison by Emily Morison Beck. Copyright © 1978 by Emily Morison Beck. Reprinted by permission of Houghton Mifflin Company and Curtis Brown Ltd.

Samuel De Champlain: Father of New France by Samuel Eliot Morison. Copyright © 1972 by Samuel Eliot Morison. Reprinted by permission of Little, Brown and Co. in association with The Atlantic Monthly Press.

Clipper Ships, *Living Again*, and *Under Sail* by Felix Riesenberg, Sr. Reprinted by permission of Felix Riesenberg III.

"On the Bowsprit" from *The Sailing Ship* by Stanley Rogers. Copyright © 1950 by Stanley Rogers. Reprinted by permission of Harper & Row, Publishers, Inc., and McIntosh and Otis, Inc.

The works of Guenther T. Schulz from *Sailing Round Cape Horn*. Reproduced courtesy of Koehlers Verlagsgesellschaft MBH, Herford, West Germany.

"The Ballad of How MacPherson Held the Floor" from *The Collected Poems of Robert Service*. Copyright 1940 by Robert Service. Copyright renewed 1967 by Germaine Service and Iris Davies. Reprinted by permission of Dodd, Mead & Company, Inc., McGraw-Hill Ryerson Limited, and Ernest Benn Limited.

Full Sail by C. Fox Smith. Reprinted by permission of Methuen & Co. Ltd.

Drawing by George Varian from *The Great Quest* by Charles Boardman Hawes. Copyright 1921, © 1949 by Charles Boardman Hawes. Reprinted by permission of Little, Brown in association with The Atlantic Monthly Press.

N.B. *The individual chapter headings were written to describe the subject matter and lend a narrative flow to the book. Footnoted on each two-page spread are the names of the contributing artist and author. All other facts, including the titles of the illustrations and selections, their sources, and other credits, are listed in the Acknowledgments section starting on page 290.*

Contents

GORDON GRANT

This book is dedicated to the

WARDEN FAMILY

who for five generations have found delight

and wonder upon the sea

FRANK W. BENSON

The Artists

Frank Weston Benson
John P. Benson
Edmund Blampied
Michael F. Blaser
Muirhead Bone
Franklin Booth
Frank Brangwyn
Arthur Briscoe
George Chinnery
Frederick E. Church
Montague Dawson
H. W. Ditzler
William Holland Drury
Kerr Eby
Anton Otto Fischer
George Gale
Lyle Galloway
William Gilkerson
Gordon Grant
Winslow Homer
Edward Hopper
Marshall Johnson
Philip Kappel
John F. Leavitt

William Lee-Hankey
Philip Little
Barry Moser
William Edward Norton
Frederick L. Owen
Howard Pyle
Richard H. Rodgers
Stanley Rogers
Frank E. Schoonover
Guenther T. Schulz
Warren Sheppard
Frank Vining Smith
Jack Spurling
John Stobart
Dwight C. Sturges
Henri de Toulouse-Lautrec
James Gale Tyler
George Edmund Varian
George Canning Wales
James Abbott McNeill Whistler
Norman Wilkinson
Rufus Fairchild Zogbaum
Anders Zorn

The Authors

Don Blanding
David Bone
Edwin James Brady
John Ross Browne
Henry Howard Brownell
Robert Browning
Robert Carse
Samuel de Champlain
George Chapman
Washington Chase
Joseph Conrad
Allan Cunningham
Richard Henry Dana, Jr.
Charles Dibdin
Anton Otto Fischer
Kenneth Grahame
Daniel Whitehead Hicky
Frederic Stanhope Hill

Washington Irving
John Paul Jones
Rudyard Kipling
Henry Wadsworth Longfellow
Tom Manners
Frederick Marryat
John Masefield
Herman Melville
Walter Mitchell
Samuel Eliot Morison
Felix Riesenberg
Robert N. Rose
Robert W. Service
Frank Hubert Shaw
C. Fox Smith
Algernon Charles Swinburne
Walt Whitman

GORDON GRANT

THE OLD PORT
G.C.W. 1929

Preface

The chroniclers of ocean voyages—writers like Dana, Conrad, Melville, and Masefield—were more often narrators than philosophers. Yet scattered through their works are statements and stories which, when taken as a whole, represent a set of life-values born of the sea. These authors viewed commerce as an honorable profession; a ship as a living creation of man; and life as risk, with achievement the hard-won reward. To them, a crew must have courage, skill, and endurance, and its captain must be intelligent, experienced, practical, principled, and enterprising—a charismatic, iron-willed, lion-hearted leader of men.

That life on the sea is different from life on land is a recurrent theme. Comparing landsmen to seamen, Edwin James Brady writes in "You and Us":

> *You had your share of doin'—*
> *You had your share to do—*
> *But you had wives for wooin',*
> *An' homes an' kiddies too.*
> *You heard the chink o' glasses,*
> *You heard the laugh o' lasses,*
> *Had time to rest and play,*
> *To let your racked souls borrow,*
> *In promise of To-Morrow,*
> *Some comfort for To-Day.*
>
> *But Us! We crouched together*
> *'Longside the weather-rail,*
> *An' saw the howlin' weather*
> *Slog down the stingin' hail;*
> *We heard dark Legions shoutin'*
> *When Davy Jones was floutin'*
> *Our souls—give up for dead.*
> *With brine-cut, bleedin' faces,*
> *We manned the weather-braces*
> *When You were safe abed.*

Finally, sailors take fierce pride in their ships. And for them the greatest of all sailing vessels were the clipper ships. "These clipper ships of the early 1850's were built of wood in shipyards from Rockland in Maine to Baltimore. Their architects, like poets who transmute nature's message into song, obeyed what wind and wave had taught them, to create the noblest of all sailing vessels, and the most beautiful creations of man in America. With no extraneous ornament except a figurehead, a bit of carving and a few lines of gold leaf, their one purpose of speed over the great ocean routes was achieved by perfect balance of spars and sails to the curving lines of the smooth black hull; and this harmony of mass, form and color was practiced to the music of dancing waves and of brave winds whistling in the rigging. These were our Gothic cathedrals, our Parthenon." It was ships like these, and their crews, which inspired our golden age of marine art and literature.

. . .

The voyages of sailors dramatize how great is man's courage, how small his wants, and how magnificent his efforts and accomplishments. To capture the spirit and zest of life aboard ship, this book combines marine art and literature, matching each page of poetry or prose with an appropriate illustration. The artists and writers represented span a period of one hundred and fifty years. Since they never collaborated, you may find an occasional inconsistency in chronology, geography, or nautical detail between words and pictures. Still, if these pages transport you to sea in an armchair, they have accomplished their task.

Together the words and pictures tell the story of a voyage, highlighting moments of fellowship, work, adventure, or danger in the lives of sailors. The time of this story is the second half of the nineteenth century. The journey is around Cape Horn to exotic China and back. The purpose—a lasting salute to the intrepid sailor and his ship.

H.W.W.

N.B. *To maintain a continuous narrative throughout the book, I have provided a chapter heading for each two-page spread, with a footnote giving the names of artists and authors. The footnote lists the artist's name first and the author's second, separated by a slash. In cases where more than one illustration or passage of prose appears on facing pages, the artists are identified from left to right and the authors in the order given.*

All other facts, including the full titles of illustrations and text selections, their sources, and other credits, are contained in the Acknowledgments section.

The Sea Belongs to Us All

The sea belongs to us all, and every aspect of it, from halcyon calm to howling hurricane, is fraught with beauty. In these pages I am trying to share with the reader what the sea has meant to me; to pass on to another generation the delight that salt water affords to those who will take the trouble to learn sea lore. To ply, unhurried, the blue deeps, or skirt the shining margents of the land, communing with the element whence life sprang, hearing no other sound but the plash of oar, the flap of sail, the whistling of wind in the rigging, and the swish and gurgle of cloven waves, revives one's strength and refreshes one's spirit. Here, the tiniest lad sailing a dinghy becomes partner to the great navigators and discoverers of history; here, too, borrowing St.-John Perse's bold metaphor, unity between earth and heaven is recovered, truth is brought to light like the flash of a steel sword blade drawn out of its sheath; and we, the guests, can share the same supper with our Host.

EDWARD HOPPER / SAMUEL ELIOT MORISON, in *Sailor Historian*   11

The Lure of the Sea

"And now," he was softly saying, "I take to the road again, holding on south-westwards for many a long and dusty day; till at last I reach the little grey sea town I know so well, that clings along one steep side of the harbour. There through dark doorways you look down flights of stone steps, overhung by great pink tufts of valerian and ending in a patch of sparkling blue water. The little boats that lie tethered to the rings and stanchions of the old sea-wall are gaily painted as those I clambered in and out of in my own childhood; the salmon leap on the flood tide, schools of mackerel flash and play past quay-sides and foreshores, and by the windows the great vessels glide, night and day, up to their moorings or forth to the open sea. There, sooner or later, the ships of all seafaring nations arrive; and there, at its destined hour, the ship of my choice will let go its anchor. I shall take my time, I shall tarry and bide, till at last the right one lies waiting for me, warped out into midstream, loaded low, her bowsprit pointing down harbour. I shall slip on board, by boat or along hawser; and then one morning I shall wake to the song and tramp of the sailors, the clink of the capstan, and the rattle of the anchor-chain coming merrily in. We shall break out the jib and the foresail, the white houses on the harbour side will glide slowly past us as she gathers steering-way, and the voyage will have begun! As she forges towards the headland she will clothe herself with canvas; and then, once outside, the sounding slap of great green seas as she heels to the wind, pointing South!

"And you, you will come too, young brother; for the days pass, and never return, and the South still waits for you. Take the Adventure, heed the call, now ere the irrevocable moment passes! 'Tis but a banging of the door behind you, a blithesome step forward, and you are out of the old life and into the new! Then some day, some day long hence, jog home here if you will, when the cup has been drained and the play has been played, and sit down by your quiet river with a store of goodly memories for company. You can easily overtake me on the road, for you are young, and I am ageing and go softly. I will linger, and look back; and at last I will surely see you coming, eager and light-hearted, with all the South in your face!"

"AWAY, YOU RIO"
G.O.W. 1929

13

In Praise of Sailors

Give me a spirit that on this life's rough sea
Loves t'have his sails fill'd with a lusty wind,
Even till his sail-yards tremble, his masts crack,
And his rapt ship run on her side so low
That she drinks water, and her keel plows air;
There is no danger to a man that knows
What life and death is; there's not any law
Exceeds his knowledge; neither is it lawful
That he should stoop to any other law.
He goes before them, and commands them all,
That to himself is a law rational.

Roadways

One road leads to London,
    One road runs to Wales,
My road leads me seawards
    To the white dipping sails.

One road leads to the river,
    As it goes singing slow;
My road leads to shipping,
    Where the bronzed sailors go.

Leads me, lures me, calls me
    To salt green tossing sea;
A road without earth's road-dust
    Is the right road for me.

A wet road heaving, shining,
    And wild with seagulls' cries,
A mad salt sea-wind blowing
    The salt spray in my eyes.

My road calls me, lures me
    West, east, south, and north;
Most roads lead men homewards,
    My road leads me forth

To add more miles to the tally
    Of grey miles left behind,
In quest of that one beauty
    God put me here to find.

To Seafaring Men
in Hopes of Good Fortune

Who seeks the way to win renown
>> *Or flies with wings of high desire;*
Who seeks to wear the laurel crown,
>> *Or hath the mind that would aspire:*
Tell him his native soil eschew,
Tell him go range and seek anew.

To pass the seas some think a toil,
>> *Some think it strange abroad to roam*
Some think it grief to leave their soil,
>> *Their parents, kinsfolk and their home;*
Think so who list, I like it not,
I must abroad and try my lot.

The Building of a Ship

"Build me straight, O worthy Master!
      Stanch and strong, a goodly vessel,
That shall laugh at all disaster,
      And with wave and whirlwind wrestle!"

The merchant's word
Delighted the Master heard;
For his heart was in his work, and the heart
Giveth grace unto every Art.
A quiet smile played round his lips,
As the eddies and dimples of the tide
Play round the bows of ships,
That steadily at anchor ride.
And with a voice that was full of glee,
He answered, "Erelong we will launch
A vessel as goodly, and strong, and staunch,
As ever weathered a wintry sea!"
And first with nicest skill and art,
Perfect and finished in every part,
A little model the Master wrought,
Which should be to the larger plan
What the child is to the man,
Its counterpart in miniature;
That with a hand more swift and sure
The greater labor might be brought
To answer to his inward thought.

Day by Day the Vessel Grew

"Thus," said he, "will we build this ship!
Lay square the blocks upon the slip,
And follow well this plan of mine.
Choose the timbers with greatest care;
Of all that is unsound beware;
For only what is sound and strong
To this vessel shall belong.
Cedar of Maine and Georgia pine
Here together shall combine.
A goodly frame, and a goodly fame,
And the UNION be her name!"

Thus with the rising of the sun
Was the noble task begun,
And soon throughout the ship-yard's bounds
Were heard the intermingled sounds
Of axes and of mallets, plied
With vigorous arms on every side;
Plied so deftly and so well,
That, ere the shadows of evening fell,
The keel of oak for a noble ship,
Scarfed and bolted, straight and strong,
Was lying ready, and stretched along
The blocks, well placed upon the slip.
Happy, thrice happy, every one
Who sees his labor well begun,
And not perplexed and multiplied,
By idly waiting for time and tide!

Day by day the vessel grew,
With timbers fashioned strong and true,
Stemson and keelson and sternson-knee,
Till, framed with perfect symmetry,
A skeleton ship rose up to view!
And around the bows and along the side
The heavy hammers and mallets plied,
Till after many a week, at length,
Wonderful for form and strength,
Sublime in its enormous bulk,
Loomed aloft the shadowy hulk!
And around it columns of smoke, upwreathing,
Rose from the boiling, bubbling, seething
Caldron, that glowed,
And overflowed
With the black tar, heated for the sheathing.
And amid the clamors
Of clattering hammers,
He who listened heard now and then
The song of the Master and his men:—

"Build me straight, O worthy Master,
    Stanch and strong, a goodly vessel,
That shall laugh at all disaster,
    And with wave and whirlwind wrestle!"

The Figurehead

And at the bows an image stood,
By a cunning artist carved in wood,
With robes of white, that far behind
Seemed to be fluttering in the wind.
It was not shaped in a classic mould,
Not like a Nymph or Goddess of old,
Or Naiad rising from the water,
But modelled from the Master's daughter!
On many a dreary and misty night,
'T will be seen by the rays of the signal light,
Speeding along through the rain and the dark,
Like a ghost in its snow-white sark,
The pilot of some phantom bark,
Guiding the vessel, in its flight,
By a path none other knows aright!

The Power and the Glory

Behold, at last,
Each tall and tapering mast
Is swung into its place;
Shrouds and stays
Holding it firm and fast!

Long ago,
In the deer-haunted forests of Maine,
When upon mountain and plain
Lay the snow,
They fell—those lordly pines!
Those grand, majestic pines!
'Mid shouts and cheers
The jaded steers,
Panting beneath the goad,
Dragged down the weary, winding road
Those captive kings so straight and tall,
To be shorn of their streaming hair,
And naked and bare,
To feel the stress and the strain
Of the wind and the reeling main,
Whose roar
Would remind them forevermore
Of their native forests they should not see again.

And everywhere
The slender, graceful spars
Poise aloft in the air,
And at the mast-head,
White, blue, and red,
A flag unrolls the stripes and stars.

UNKNOWN / HENRY WADSWORTH LONGFELLOW

The Launching

Decked with flags and streamers gay,
In honor of her marriage day,
Her snow-white signals fluttering, blending,
Round her like a veil descending,
Ready to be
The bride of the gray old sea.

. . .

All is finished! and at length
Has come the bridal day
Of beauty and of strength.
To-day the vessel shall be launched!
With fleecy clouds the sky is blanched,
And o'er the bay,
Slowly, in all his splendors dight,
The great sun rises to behold the sight.
The ocean old,
Centuries old,
Strong as youth, and as uncontrolled,
Paces restless to and fro,
Up and down the sands of gold.
His beating heart is not at rest;
And far and wide,
With ceaseless flow,
His beard of snow
Heaves with the heaving of his breast.
He waits impatient for his bride.
There she stands,
With her foot upon the sands,

The worthy pastor—
The shepherd of that wandering flock,
That has the ocean for its wold,
That has the vessel for its fold,
Leaping ever from rock to rock—
Spake, with accents mild and clear,
Words of warning, words of cheer . . .
Then the Master,
With a gesture of command,
Waved his hand;
And at the word,
Loud and sudden there was heard,
All around them and below,
The sound of hammers, blow on blow,
Knocking away the shores and spurs.
And see! she stirs!
She starts,—she moves,—she seems to feel
The thrill of life along her keel,
And, spurning with her foot the ground,
With one exulting, joyous bound,
She leaps into the ocean's arms!

Wanderlust

A wind's in the heart of me, a fire's in my heels,
I am tired of brick and stone and rumbling wagon-wheels;
I hunger for the sea's edge, the limits of the land,
Where the wild old Atlantic is shouting on the sand.

Oh I'll be going, leaving the noises of the street,
To where a lifting foresail-foot is yanking at the sheet;
To a windy, tossing anchorage where yawls and ketches ride,
Oh I'll be going, going, until I meet the tide.

And first I'll hear the sea-wind, the mewing of the gulls,
The clucking, sucking of the sea about the rusty hulls,
The songs at the capstan in the hooker warping out,
And then the heart of me'll know I'm there or thereabout.

Oh I am tired of brick and stone, the heart of me is sick,
For windy green, unquiet sea, the realm of Moby Dick;
And I'll be going, going, from the roaring of the wheels,
For a wind's in the heart of me, a fire's in my heels.

Yarn of a Former Jolly Roger—1

We were schooner-rigged and rakish, with a long and lissome hull,
And we flew the pretty colours of the cross-bones and the skull;
We'd a big black Jolly Roger flapping grimly at the fore,
And we sailed the Spanish Water in the happy days of yore.

JAMES A. MCNEILL WHISTLER / JOHN MASEFIELD

Yarn of a Former Jolly Roger - II

We'd a long brass gun amidships,
    like a well conducted ship,
We had each a brace of pistols
    and a cutlass at the hip;

It's a point which tells against us,
   and a fact to be deplored,
But we chased the goodly merchant-men
   and laid their ships aboard.

Yarn of a Former Jolly Roger – III

Then the dead men fouled the scuppers and the wounded filled the chains,
And the paint-work all was spatter-dashed with other people's brains,
She was boarded, she was looted, she was scuttled till she sank,
And the pale survivors left us by the medium of the plank.

O! then it was (while standing by the taffrail on the poop)
We could hear the drowning folk lament the absent chicken-coop;
Then, having washed the blood away, we'd little else to do
Than to dance a quiet hornpipe as the old salts taught us to.

O! the fiddle on the fo'c's'le, and the slapping naked soles,
And the genial "Down the middke, Jake, and curtsey when she rolls!"
With the silver seas around us and the pale moon overhead,
And the look-out not a-looking and his pipe-bowl glowing red.

Ah! the pig-tailed, quidding pirates and the pretty pranks we played,
All have since been put a stop-to by the naughty Board of Trade;
The schooners and the merry crews are laid away to rest,
A little south the sunset in the Islands of the Blest.

The Sea-Wife

There dwells a wife by the Northern Gate,
    And a wealthy wife is she;
She breeds a breed o' rovin' men
    And casts them over sea.

And some are drowned in deep water,
    And some in sight o' shore,
And word goes back to the weary wife
    And ever she sends more.

For since that wife had gate or gear,
    Or hearth or garth or field,
She willed her sons to the white harvest,
    And that is a bitter yield.

She wills her sons to the wet ploughing,
    To ride the horse of tree,
And syne her sons come back again
    Far-spent from out the sea.

The good wife's sons come home again
    With little into their hands,
But the lore of men that ha' dealt with men
    In the new and naked lands;

But the faith of men that have brothered men
    By more than easy breath,
And the eyes o' men that have read with men
    In the open books of Death.

Rich are they, rich in wonders seen,
    But poor in the goods o' men;
So what they ha' got by the skin of their teeth
    They sell for their teeth again.

For whether they lose to the naked life
    Or win to their hearts' desire,
They tell it all to the weary wife
    That nods beside the fire.

Her hearth is wide to every wind
    That makes the white ash spin;
And tide and tide and 'tween the tides
    Her sons go out and in;

(Out with great mirth that do desire
    Hazard of trackless ways,
In with content to wait their watch
    And warm before the blaze);

And some return by failing light,
    And some in waking dream,
For she hears the heels of the dripping ghosts
    That ride the rough roof-beam.

Home, they come home from all the ports,
    The living and the dead;
The good wife's sons come home again
    For her blessing on their head!

Up Anchor and Away to Rio

Oh— say was you ev - er in   Ri - o Grande: Way, —you Ri - o. Oh,

wa - s you ev - er o — n   that strand?   For we're bound to the Ri — o

Grande: And a — w — a — y Ri — o,   Way— you Ri - o,   Sing

fare ye well my bon-ny young girls, For we're bound to the Ri - o   Grande.

Oh, New York town is no place for me;
    Way, you Rio!
I'll pack up my bag and go to sea,

Now, you Bowery ladies, we'll let you know,
    Way, you Rio!
We're bound to the south' ard–O Lord, let her go!

We'll sell our salt cod for molasses and rum,
    Way, you Rio!
And get home again 'fore Thanksgiving has come.

Sing good-by to Nellie and good-by to Sue,
    Way, you Rio!
And you who are listening, good-by to you.

CHORUS

For we're bound to the Rio Grande:
And away, Rio,
Way, you Rio,
Sing fare ye well my bonny young girls
For we're bound to the Rio Grande.

Setting Forth–1

The Paddle-tug Wrestler *arrived at an hour ere flood,*
Then slowly the hawser was passt and the mooring ropes slackt,
The ship moved away from her berthing, her voyage begun.

In dock, near her berth, lay the famous American ship
The R.D. Rice, lofty and lovely, with three skysail yards.
Her captain, there watching the Wanderer *passing to sea,*
Cried to George Currie, "I'll bet you a rosy-cheekt apple
I'll be in San 'Frisco before you": the Wanderers laught
From pride in their racer now trembling to gallop the sea.

Slowly she moved to the gateway that led to the river;
The gates were wide opened, beyond lay the fullness of flood.
There on the pierhead, the dock-gate officials and riggers,
The stevedoors and dockers and penniless seamen were buncht
Watching her ripples advance as she followed her tug.

Now as that queen of the water went out to her kingdom,
As spear-like for diving the spike of her jib-boom was poised
Over the paddle churn foam slapping weeds at the dock gates,
And slowly her gazing white woman moved forward in thought
Between the stone walls, and her boys, coiling gear, paused to watch,
A man of that muster of dockers went up to the edge,
And took off his cap with, "Three cheers for the Wanderer*": then*
All of those sea-beaten fellows swung caps, and their cheering
Sent the gulls mewing aloft: then George Shearer, the chief mate,
Up on her fo'c'sle, replied with "Three cheers for Pierhead, boys."
The boys and the seamen all swinging caps shouted three cheers.
A man from the pierhead jumpt into the rigging aboard.
She passt in procession of masts through the narrow dock gates.

Setting Forth–II

Now in the river she paused as she swung through her quadrant;
Men hurried to watch her as slowly she headed for sea,
At bidding extending her loitering length of delight.
All of the power of muscle of hundreds of builders
Beating out iron and steel into straightness or curving,
All of the knowledge and cunning of hundreds of thinkers
Who make from the stubborn the swanlike and sweeping and swift,
All of the art of the brain that had seen her in vision,
Had gone to the making her perfect in beauty and strength.
Her black painted ports above black showed the curve of her sheer,
Her yellow masts raked as they rose with their burden of yards.
High, high aloft rose her skysails, and over her skysails
Bright in the sun, blowing out, blue and white, were her colours.

Casting Off

A slight haze blurred the horizon. Outside the harbor the measureless expanse of smooth water lay sparkling like a floor of jewels, and as empty as the sky. The short black tug gave a pluck to windward, in the usual way, then let go the rope, and hovered for a moment on the quarter with her engines stopped; while the slim, long hull of the ship moved ahead slowly under lower topsails. The loose upper canvas blew out in the breeze with soft round contours, resembling small white clouds snared in the maze of ropes. Then the sheets were hauled home, the yards hoisted, and the ship became a high and lonely pyramid, gliding, all shining and white, through the sunlit mist. The tug turned short round and went away towards the land. Twenty-six pairs of eyes watched her low broad stern crawling languidly over the smooth swell between the two paddlewheels that turned fast, beating the water with fierce hurry. She resembled an enormous and aquatic blackbeetle, surprised by the light, overwhelmed by the sunshine, trying to escape with ineffectual effort into the distant gloom of the land. She left a lingering smudge of smoke on the sky, and two vanishing trails of foam on the water. On the place where she had stopped a round black patch of soot remained, undulating on the swell—an unclean mark of the creature's rest.

The Circling Sea

The *Narcissus* left alone, heading south, seemed to stand resplendent and still upon the restless sea, under the moving sun. Flakes of foam swept past her sides; the water struck her with flashing blows; the land glided away, slowly fading; a few birds screamed on motionless wings over the swaying mastheads. But soon the land disappeared, the birds went away; . . . the ship's wake, long and straight, stretched itself out through a day of immense solitude. The setting sun, burning on the level of the water, flamed crimson below the blackness of heavy rain clouds. The sunset squall, coming up from behind, dissolved itself into the short deluge of a hissing shower. It left the ship glistening from trucks to waterline, and with darkened sails. She ran easily before a fair breeze, with her decks cleared for the night; and, moving along with her, was heard the sustained and monotonous swishing of the waves, mingled with the low whispers of men mustered aft for the setting of watches; the short plaint of some block aloft; or, now and then, a loud sigh of wind.

The passage had begun, and the ship, a fragment detached from the earth, went on lonely and swift like a small planet. Round her the abysses of sky and sea met in an unattainable frontier. A great circular solitude moved with her, ever changing and ever the same, always monotonous and always imposing. Now and then another wandering white speck, burdened with life, appeared far off—disappeared; intent on its own destiny.

Like the Eagle Free

A wet sheet and a flowing sea,
  A wind that follows fast
And fills the white and rustling sail
  And bends the gallant mast;
And bends the gallant mast, my boys,
  While like the eagle free
Away the good ship flies, and leaves
  Old England by the lee.

O for a soft and gentle wind!
  I heard a fair one cry;
But give to me the snoring breeze
  And white waves heaving high;
And white waves heaving high, my lads,
  The good ship tight and free—
The world of waters is our home,
  The merry men are we.

There's tempest in yon hornèd moon,
  And lightning in yon cloud;
But hark the music, mariners!
  The wind is piping loud;
The wind is piping loud, my boys,
  The lightning flashes free—
While the hollow oak our palace is,
  Our heritage the sea.

51

　MONTAGUE DAWSON / JOSEPH CONRAD

The Setting Sun

The West Wind reigns over the seas surrounding the coasts of these kingdoms; and from the gateways of the channels, from promontories as if from watchtowers, from estuaries of rivers as if from postern gates, from passage-ways, inlets, straits, firths, the garrison of the Isle and the crews of the ships going and returning look to the westward to judge by the varied splendours of his sunset mantle the mood of that arbitrary ruler. The end of the day is the time to gaze at the kingly face of the Westerly Weather, who is the arbiter of ships' destinies. Benignant and splendid, or splendid and sinister, the western sky reflects the hidden purposes of the royal mind. Clothed in a mantle of dazzling gold or draped in rags of black clouds like a beggar, the might of the Westerly Wind sits enthroned upon the western horizon with the whole North Atlantic as a footstool for his feet and the first twinkling stars making a diadem for his brow. Then the seamen, attentive courtiers of the weather, think of regulating the conduct of their ships by the mood of the master. The West Wind is too great a king to be a dissembler: he is no calculator plotting deep schemes in a sombre heart; he is too strong for small artifices; there is passion in all his moods, even in the soft mood of his serene days, in the grace of his blue sky whose immense and unfathomable tenderness reflected in the mirror of the sea embraces, possesses, lulls to sleep the ships with white sails. He is all things to all oceans; he is like a poet seated upon a throne—magnificent, simple, barbarous, pensive, generous, impulsive, changeable, unfathomable—but when you understand him, always the same. Some of his sunsets are like pageants devised for the delight of the multitude, when all the gems of the royal treasure-house are displayed above the sea. Others are like the opening of his royal confidence, tinged with thoughts of sadness and compassion in a melancholy splendour meditating upon the short-lived peace of the waters. And I have seen him put the pent-up anger of his heart into the aspect of the inaccessible sun, and cause it to glare fiercely like the eye of an implacable autocrat out of a pale and frightened sky.

The Kingdom of the Wind

The winds of North and South are but small princes amongst the powers of the sea. They have no territory of their own; they are not reigning winds anywhere. Yet it is from their houses that the reigning dynasties which have shared between them the waters of the earth are sprung. All the weather of the world is based upon the contest of the Polar and Equatorial strains of that tyrannous race. The West Wind is the greatest king. The East rules between the Tropics. They have shared each ocean between them. Each has his genius of supreme rule. The King of the West never intrudes upon the recognized dominion of his kingly brother. He is a barbarian, of a northern type. Violent without craftiness, and furious without malice, one may imagine him seated masterfully with a double-edged sword on his knees upon the painted and gilt clouds of the sunset, bowing his shock head of golden locks, a flaming beard over his breast, imposing, colossal, mighty-limbed, with a thundering voice, distended cheeks, and fierce blue eyes, urging the speed of his gales. The other, the East King, the king of blood-red sunrises, I represent to myself as a spare Southerner with clear-cut features, black-browed and dark-eyed, grey-robed, upright in sunshine, resting a smooth-shaven cheek in the palm of his hand, impenetrable, secret, full of wiles, fine-drawn, keen—meditating aggressions.

The West Wind keeps faith with his brother the King of the Easterly Weather. "What we have divided we have divided," he seems to say in his gruff voice, this ruler without guile, who hurls as if in sport enormous masses of cloud across the sky, and flings the great waves of the Atlantic clear across from the shores of the New World upon the hoary headlands of Old Europe, which harbours more kings and rulers upon its seamed and furrowed body than all the oceans of the world together. "What we have divided we have divided; and if no rest and peace in this world have fallen to my share, leave me alone. Let me play at quoits with cyclonic gales, flinging the discs of spinning cloud and whirling air from one end of my dismal kingdom to the other: over the Great Banks or along the edges of pack-ice—this one with true aim right into the bight of the Bay of Biscay, that other upon the fiords of Norway, across the North Sea where the fishermen of many nations look watchfully into my angry eye. This is the time of kingly sport."

And the royal master of high latitudes sighs mightily, with the sinking sun upon his breast and the double-edged sword upon his knees, as if wearied by the innumerable centuries of a strenuous rule and saddened by the unchangeable aspect of the ocean under his feet—by the endless vista of future ages where the work of sowing the wind and reaping the whirlwind shall go on and on till his realm of living waters becomes a frozen and motionless ocean. But the other, crafty and unmoved, nursing his shaven chin between the thumb and forefinger of his slim and treacherous hand, thinks deep within his heart full of guile: "Aha! our brother of the West has fallen into the mood of kingly melancholy. He is tired of playing with circular gales, and blowing great guns, and unrolling thick streamers of fog in wanton sport at the cost of his own poor, miserable subjects. Their fate is most pitiful. Let us make a foray upon the dominions of that noisy barbarian, a great raid from Finisterre to Hatteras, catching his fishermen unawares, baffling the fleets that trust to his power, and shooting sly arrows into the livers of men who court his good graces. He is, indeed, a worthless fellow." And forthwith, while the West Wind meditates upon the vanity of his irresistible might, the thing is done, and the Easterly Weather sets in upon the North Atlantic.

The prevailing weather of the North Atlantic is typical of the way in which the West Wind rules his realm on which the sun never sets. North Atlantic is the heart of a great empire. It is the part of the West Wind's dominions most thickly populated with generations of fine ships and hardy men. Heroic deeds and adventurous exploits have been performed there, within the very stronghold of his sway. The best sailors in the world have been born and bred under the shadow of his sceptre, learning to manage their ships with skill and audacity before the steps of his stormy throne. Reckless adventurers, toiling fishermen, admirals as wise and brave as the world has ever known have waited upon the signs of his Westerly sky. Fleets of victorious ships have hung upon his breath. He has tossed in his hand squadrons of war-scarred three-deckers, and shredded out in mere sport the bunting of flags hallowed in the traditions of honour and glory. He is a good friend and a dangerous enemy, without mercy to unseaworthy ships and faint-hearted seamen. In his kingly way he has taken but little account of lives sacrificed to his impulsive policy; he is a king with a double-edged sword bared in his right hand. The East Wind, an interloper in the dominions of Westerly Weather, is an impassive-faced tyrant with a sharp poniard held behind his back for a treacherous stab.

W-3345
Keppel

The Helmsman

When, with the gale at her heel, the ship lies down and recovers—
Rolling through forty degrees, combing the stars with her tops,
What says the man at the wheel, holding her straight as she hovers
On the summits of wind-screening seas; studying her as she drops?

Behind him the blasts without check from the Pole to the Tropic, pursue him,
Heaving up, heaping high, slamming home, the surges he must not regard:
Beneath him the crazy wet deck, and all Ocean on end to undo him:
Above him one desperate sail, thrice-reefed but still buckling the yard!

Under his hand fleet the spokes and return, to be held or set free again;
And she bows and makes shift to obey their behest, till the master-wave comes
And her gunnel goes under in thunder and smokes, and she chokes in the
   trough of the sea again—
Ere she can lift and make way to its crest; and he, as he nurses her, hums! . . .

These have so utterly mastered their work that they work without thinking;
Holding three-fifths of their brain in reserve for whatever betide.
So, when catastrophe threatens, of colic, collision or sinking,
They shunt the full gear into train, and take that small thing in their stride.

The "Old Man"

Let every commander keep before him this eternal truth, that to be well obeyed he must be perfectly esteemed.

.   .   .

Never had I met a more generous and warm hearted man. He was kind to his crew, respected their feelings and did all in his power to promote their comfort. At the same time he preserved discipline and made every man know his place. A better sailor never walked a ship's planks. He understood his duty from beginning to end, kept within the bounds of authority, and, while faithful to the interests of the owners, gave the crew their full complement of provisions, and encouraged them in all their enjoyments. The consequence was that they respected him, and made themselves active and useful. Brave, energetic and liberal, he set an example that excited the emulation of all on board. No man flinched from danger, avoided work, or refused to share the best he had with his shipmates.

Collision

We one day descried some shapeless object drifting at a distance. At sea, everything that breaks the monotony of the surrounding expanse attracts attention. It proved to be the mast of a ship that must have been completely wrecked, for there were the remains of handkerchiefs, by which some of the crew had fastened themselves to this spar, to prevent their being washed off by the waves. There was no trace by which the name of the ship could be ascertained. The wreck had evidently drifted about for many months; clusters of shell-fish had fastened about it, and long sea-weeds flaunted at its sides. But where, thought I, is the crew?

Their struggle has long been over—they have gone down amidst the roar of the tempest—their bones lie whitening among the caverns of the deep. Silence, oblivion, like the waves, have closed over them, and no one can tell the story of their end. What sighs have been wafted after that ship; what prayers offered up at the desired fireside of home! How often has the mistress, the wife, the mother, pored over the daily news, to catch some casual intelligence of this rover of the deep! How has expectation darkened into anxiety—anxiety into dread—and dread into despair! Alas! not one memento shall ever return for love to cherish. All that shall ever be known, is that she sailed from her port, "and was never heard of more!"

The sight of this wreck, as usual, gave rise to many dismal anecdotes. This was particularly the case in the evening, when the weather, which had hitherto been fair, began to look wild and threatening, and gave indications of one of those sudden storms that will sometimes break in upon the serenity of a summer voyage. As we sat round the dull light of a lamp, in the cabin, that made the gloom more ghastly, every one had his tale of shipwreck and disaster. I was particularly struck with a short one related by the captain:

"As I was once sailing," said he, "in a fine, stout ship, across the banks of Newfoundland, one of those heavy fogs that prevail in those parts rendered it impossible for us to see far ahead, even in the daytime; but at night the weather was so thick that we could not distinguish any object at twice the length of the ship. I kept lights at the mast-head, and a constant watch forward to look out for fishing smacks which are accustomed to lie at anchor on the banks. The wind was blowing a smacking breeze, and we were going at a great rate through the water. Suddenly the watch gave the alarm of 'a sail a-head!'—it was scarcely uttered before we were upon her. She was a small schooner, at anchor, with a broad-side toward us. The crew were all asleep, and had neglected to hoist a light. We struck her just amid-ships. The force, the size, the weight of our vessel, bore her down below the waves; we passed over her and were hurried on our course. As the crashing wreck was sinking beneath us, I had glimpse of two or three half-naked wretches, rushing from her cabin; they just started from their beds to be swallowed shrieking by the waves. I heard their drowning cry mingling with the wind. The blast that bore it to our ears, swept us all out of all farther hearing. I shall never forget the cry! It was some time before we could put the ship about, she was under such headway. We returned as nearly as we could guess, to the place where the smack had anchored. We cruised about for several hours in the dense fog. We fired signal-guns, and listened if we might hear the halloo of any survivors; but all was silent—we never saw or heard anything of them more."

GEORGE C. WALES / WASHINGTON IRVING 61

Destinations

Names! The lure in names of places
Stirring thoughts of foreign faces,
Ports and palaces and steamers.
Names are ships to carry dreamers.

    Pago-pago, Suva, Java,
    Languor, lotuses and lava,
Everything a dreamer wishes,
Buried treasure, flying fishes,
Cocoanuts and kings and corals,
Pirates, pearls and pagan morals,
Rum and reefs and Christian teaching,
Gin, and jungle parrots screeching.

    Kobe, Nikko, Yokohama,
    Views of sacred Fujiyama,
Bales of silk and bowls of lacquer,
Dragons on a sugar cracker,
Temples high on pictured mountains,
Purple gold-fish, perfume fountains,
Amber, obis, geisha dances,
Almond eyes and slanted glances.

    Places that I pray I may go,
    Rio, Terra del Fuego,
Condors soaring in the Andes,
Cloying Guatemalan candies,

Pampas grasses, pink flamingos,
Spanish girls who call us "gringos,"
Llamas, lizards, smoking craters,
Armadillos, alligators.

    Every name a ship with cargo,
    Brass from Burmah, wheat from Fargo,
Pots and prunes and precious metal
Mined on Popocatapetl,
Chests of carved and stained catalpa,
Letters from Tegucigalpa,
Linen from an Irish shanty
For a store in Ypsilanti.

    Sailing ship and ocean liner
    Bringing stuff from Asia Minor,
Ferry boat or lazy freighter,
Folks from China or Decatur,
Mozambique or Madagascar,
Slav or Serb or savage Lascar,
Barber, Berber or Brazilian
Clad in blue or bright vermilion.

    Fascinating names of places
    Stirring thoughts of foreign faces,
    Ports and palaces and steamers,
    Names are ships to carry dreamers.

Songfest

The Captain stood on the carronade—"First lieutenant," says he,
"Send all my merry men aft here, for they must list to me:
I haven't the gift of the gab, my sons—because I'm bred to the sea;
That ship there is a Frenchman, who means to fight with we.
Odds blood, hammer and tongs, long as I've been to sea,
I've fought 'gainst every odds—but I've gain'd the victory.

"That ship there is a Frenchman, and if we don't take she,
'Tis a thousand bullets to one, that she will capture we;
I haven't the gift of the gab, my boys; so each man to his gun;
If she's not mine in half an hour, I'll flog each mother's son.
Odds bobs, hammer and tongs, long as I've been to sea,
I've fought 'gainst every odds—and I've gain'd the victory."

We fought for twenty minutes, when the Frenchmen had enough;
"I little thought," said he, "that your men were of such stuff;"
The captain took the Frenchman's sword, a low bow made to he;
"I haven't the gift of the gab, monsieur, but polite I wish to be.
Odds bobs, hammer and tongs, long as I've been to sea,
I've fought 'gainst every odds—and I've gain'd the victory."

Our captain sent for all of us; "My merry men," said he,
"I haven't the gift of the gab, my lads, but yet I thankful be;
You've done your duty handsomely, each man stood to his gun;
If you hadn't, you villains, as sure as day, I'd have
     flogg'd each mother's son.
Odds bobs, hammer and tongs, as long as I'm at sea,
I'll fight 'gainst every odds—and I'll gain the victory."

Heaving the Lead–1

For harbor, when with favoring gale,
Our clipper ship up channel steered,
And scudding under easy sail,
The high blue western lands appeared,
To heave the lead the seaman sprang,
And to the pilot cheerly sang,
    "By the deep—Nine."

And bearing up to gain the port,
Some well-known object kept in view,
A Spanish church, a ruined fort,
A beacon to the vessel true;
While oft the lead the seaman flung,
And to the pilot cheerly sung,
    "By the mark—Seven."

And as the lush-green shores we near,
We can discern the swaying palm,
The beach with azure waters clear,
The lazy heat's infectious balm.
The lead once more the seaman flung,
And to the watchful pilot sung,
    "Quarter less—Five."

GORDON GRANT, WILLIAM H. DRURY / CHARLES DIBDIN, ADAPTED BY HERBERT WARDEN

67

Heaving the Lead–II

Now to her berth the ship draws nigh,
With slackened sail she feels the tide,
Stand clear the cable is the cry,
The anchor's gone, we safely ride.
The watch is set, and through the night,
We hear the seaman with delight
Proclaim—"All's well."

PHILIP KAPPEL, GORDON GRANT / HERBERT WARDEN

Bumboats

From the quays within the town
And the coves around the bay
Came the bumboats with their produce
Plucked from off the island trees,
Hawking mangoes, coconuts and cloth,
Bananas, palm hats and live chickens—
Enough fresh victuals for a fortnight,
To be picked by a pointed finger,
Priced in sign language, and
Sold with the nod of the head
And a few tossed coins.

WILLIAM H. DRURY, PHILIP KAPPEL / JOHN MASEFIELD

Port of Call

In the harbour, in the island, in the Spanish Seas,
Are the tiny white houses and the orange trees,
And day-long, night-long, the cool and pleasant breeze
    Of the steady Trade Winds blowing.

There is the red wine; the nutty Spanish ale,
The shuffle of the dancers, the old salt's tale,
The squeaking fiddle, and the soughing in the sail
    Of the steady Trade Winds blowing.

And o' nights there's fire-flies and the yellow moon,
And in the ghostly palm-trees the sleepy tune
Of the quiet voice calling me, the long low croon
    Of the steady Trade Winds blowing.

Let's Give the Girls a Treat

Oh yesterday, I t'ink it was, while cruisin' down the street,
I met with Bill.—"Hullo," he says, "let's give the girls a treat."
We'd red bandanas round our necks 'n' our shrouds new rattled down,
So we filled a couple of Santy Cruz and cleared for Sailor Town.

We scooted south with a press of sail till we fetched to a caboose,
The "Sailor's Rest," by Dago Tom, alongside "Paddy's Goose."
Red curtains to the windies, ay, 'n' white sand to the floor,
And an old blind fiddler liltin' the tune of "Lowlands no more."

He played the "Shaking of the Sheets" 'n' the couples did advance,
Bowing, stamping, curtsying, in the shuffling of the dance;
The old floor rocked and quivered, so it struck beholders dumb,
'N' arterwards there was sweet songs 'n' good Jamaikey rum.

'N' there was many a merry yarn of many a merry spree
Aboard the ships with royals set a-sailing on the sea,
Yarns of the hooker, "Spindrift," her as had the clipper-bow—
"There ain't no ships," says Bill to me, "like that there hooker now."

When the old blind fiddler played the tune of "Pipe the Watch Below,"
The skew-eyed landlord dowsed the glim and bade us "stamp 'n' go,"
'N' we linked it home, did Bill 'n' I, adown the scattered streets,
Until we fetched to Land o' Nod atween the linen sheets.

R.F. Zogbaum
91

Harbor Race

The next morning Captain Reeder spoke to me briefly. "Do you think you can give the limeys a beating?" he asked. I remember saying something about being ready. "All right, coxon. After breakfast—and don't eat too much—row over to that coast defense ship, the Polyphemus, and toss oars."

An hour after breakfast my crew ready, we rowed leisurely, coming in close, to HMS Polyphemus, a coast defense ram. The gig stroked easily; we headed for the port gangway, then swerved, and I put her under the bow of the Britisher. The people on the deck of the man-of-war had been watching us, expecting a messenger as there was no officer in the boat. When we cut forward I gave the yoke lines a tug, swinging sharply to starboard, and called "*Oars!*" The six long dripping blades trimmed flat, and then, when under her Union Jack, I gave the loud terse command, "*Toss—oars!*" Six dripping blades sprang upright; it seemed as if we had slapped the face of old Britannia. Tossing oars under the bow of a ship is the challenge for a race, an immediate race.

On board the Britisher there was electric activity. Pipes shrilled. Officers were coming up to the quarter deck. Men were running. Then the hoarse call of "*Away-first whaler!*" Red-faced blue jackets were tumbling into a boat. We heard the clatter of oars and the click of blocks as her falls lowered smartly. The boat hit the water with a splash, a beautiful fair-modeled hull. The officer of the deck stood on the gangway grating giving instructions to her coxswain. A voice hailed, "Lay alongside, coxswain!"

"Start is from line abreast the starboard boat boom, at 'oars.' Go when you hear a shot. Do you understand?"

"Aye, aye, sir. Where to?" I called.

"To the end of the mole, round our launch." We saw her steam pinnace puffing away toward the mole, carrying a flag. "Then back to the start abreast of our boom. Are you ready?"

"Ready, sir!" The British coxswain also answered "Ready, sir!"

We were set. Both boats dipped oars and drifted to position. I spoke to my crew. "They look tough. I'll trail them for the first mile. Then, you mugs, you will have to row. Off jumpers!" The boys suddenly slid in their oars, catching the handles under the thwart stringers. Duck jumpers came off and were tossed into the bow. Six young, hard, bronzed torsos gleamed. The coxswain of the British boat looked at us, face stern. He was awaiting the order to take off jumpers, but it did not come. We looked like schoolboys on that fresh early morning. The course would be close to four miles. "Stand by!" I called. A shot cracked. "'Way—*together!*" Both boats got off clean. We shot ahead, being lighter. The stroke was high. I lowered it. The British boat got her way. They were out to slaughter us. We had a look at them—it always heartens the crew to see the other boat. Our stroke eased after the first eighth mile. The Polyphemuses crept up on us. For another eighth we rowed abreast, watching them.

"Now, boys, keep set." We were rowing against a seasoned crew, a beautiful crew. They swung their sweeps with precision. In their jumpers they looked like a toy boat propelled mechanically. I kept encouraging our fellows, who could hear the boat but could not see her. The gap widened, a half-boat length, a boat length. We were nearing the launch at the mole. "*Now*—step her up!" Quicker, quicker, the other coxswain matching us, beat for beat, we closed the gap. The work was killing. "Everything—*give everything!*" We came to the launch, abreast, the launch crew cheering. Harbor craft had gathered. People were crowding on the mole, yelling. Our ship was far away. We were going back. The limey crew were a few feet ahead of us. They hung there. As we eased, they eased. Then they began to hit it up, *up, up!* And we followed. Men could not stand that pace; they eased. "Now, mugs. *Kill 'em!*" Our boys, glistening with sweat, their young faces set hard, their lips like tight-closed traps, bent on their oars, the beautiful rhythm of bodies, arms and legs swinging to the quick sharp dip of the blades, the gig leaping. We raced and rode abreast of the Britisher. Seeing them again threw the last ounce of vim into our boys. The stroke was murdering. We drove ahead; they clung. The Polyphemus was a half-mile away. Their coxswain was urging his men. They would make the final effort, the last heart-bursting strokes. Their launch was running abreast of them, the coxswain shouting. Harbor launches and boats from ships in port were clustered to see the finish.

Breaths short, chests heaving, arms tense, my crew gave them the St Mary's finish. Faster, faster, a rapid run of spurts dropped into the last long powerful stroke, with oars bending, blades flashing. The beat was held as we stretched out the distance between us, streaming across the finish line three lengths ahead of the straining Britishers. An incredible cheer greeted us. . . .

After the Race

Your nose is a red jelly, your mouth's a toothless wreck,
And I'm atop of you, banging your head upon the dirty deck;
And both your eyes are bunged and blind like those of a mewling pup,
For you're the juggins who caught the crab and lost the ship the Cup.

He caught a crab in the spurt home, this blushing cherub did,
And the "Craigie's" whaler slipped ahead like a cart-wheel on the skid,
And beat us fair by a boat's nose though we sweated fit to start her,
So we are playing at Nero now, and he's the Christian martyr.

And Stroke is lashing a bunch of keys to the buckle-end a belt,
And we're going to lay you over a chest and baste you till you melt.
The "Craigie" boys are beating the bell and cheering down the tier,
D'ye hear, you Port Mahone baboon, I ask you, do you hear?

The Battle's Joined

Maloney watched the battle, and his brows were bleakly set,
While with him paused and panted his Hibernian Quartette
For sure it is an evil spite, and breaking to the heart,
For Irishmen to watch a fight and not be taking part.
Then suddenly on high he soared, and tightened up his belt
"And shall we see them crush," he roared, "a brother and a Celt?
A fellow artiste *needs our aid. Come on, boys, take a hand."*
Then down into the mêlée *dashed Maloney and his band.*

Fever Ship

There'll be no weepin' gells ashore when our ship sails,
Nor no crews cheerin' us, standin' at the rails,
'N' no Blue Peter a-foul the royal stay,
For we've the Yellow Fever—Harry died to-day.—
      It's cruel when a fo'c's'le gets the fever!

'N' Dick has got the fever-shakes, 'n' look what I was told
(I went to get a sack for him to keep him from the cold):
"Sir, can I have a sack?" I says, "for Dick 'e's fit to die."
"Oh, sack be shot!" the skipper says, "jest let the rotter lie!"—
      It's cruel when a fo'c's'le gets the fever!

It's a cruel port is Santos, and a hungry land,
With rows o' graves already dug in yonder strip of sand,
'N' Dick is hollerin' up the hatch, 'e says 'e's goin' blue,
His pore teeth are chattering, 'n' what's a man to do?—
      It's cruel when a fo'c's'le gets the fever!

Fever Talk–1

Spanish waters, Spanish waters, you are ringing in my ears,
Like a slow sweet piece of music from the grey forgotten years;
Telling tales, and beating tunes, and bringing weary thoughts to me
Of the sandy beach at Muertos, where I would that I could be.

There's a surf breaks on Los Muertos, and it never stops to roar,
And it's there we came to anchor, and it's there we went ashore,
Where the blue lagoon is silent amid snags of rotting trees,
Dropping like the clothes of corpses cast up by the seas.

We anchored at Los Muertos when the dipping sun was red,
We left her half-a-mile to sea, to west of Nigger Head;
And before the mist was on the Cay, before the day was done,
We were all ashore on Muertos with the gold that we had won.

We bore it through the marshes in a half-score battered chests,
Sinking, in the sucking quagmires, to the sunburn on our breasts,
Heaving over tree-trunks, gasping, damning at the flies and heat,
Longing for a long drink, out of silver, in the ship's cool lazareet.

Fever Talk- II

The moon came white and ghostly as we laid the treasure down,
There was gear there'd make a beggarman as rich as Lima Town,
Copper charms and silver trinkets from the chests of Spanish crews,
Gold doubloons and double moydores, louis d'ors and portagues,

Clumsy yellow-metal earrings from the Indians of Brazil,
Uncut emeralds out of Rio, bezoar stones from Guayaquil;
Silver, in the crude and fashioned, pots of old Arica bronze,
Jewels from the bones of Incas desecrated by the Dons.

We smoothed the place with mattocks, and we took and blazed the tree,
Which marks yon where the gear is hid that none will ever see,
And we laid aboard the ship again, and south away we steers,
Through the loud surf of Los Muertos which is beating in my ears.

I'm the last alive that knows it. All the rest have gone their ways
Killed, or died, or come to anchor in the old Mulatas Cays,
And I go singing, fiddling, old and starved and in despair,
And I know where all that gold is hid, if I were only there.

It's not the way to end it all. I'm old, and nearly blind,
And an old man's past's a strange thing, for it never leaves his mind.
And I see in dreams, awhiles, the beach, the sun's disc dipping red,
And the tall ship, under topsails, swaying in past Nigger Head.

I'd be glad to step ashore there. Glad to take a pick and go
To the lone blazed coco-palm tree in the place no others know,
And lift the gold and silver that has mouldered there for years
By the loud surf of Los Muertos which is beating in my ears.

Anchor's Aweigh!

How do we know, when the port-fog holds us
    Moored and helpless, a mile from the pier,
And the week-long summer smother enfolds us—
    How do we know it is going to clear?
There is no break in the blindfold weather,
    But, one and another, about the bay,
The unseen capstans clink together,
    Getting ready to up and away.
A pennon whimpers—the breeze has found us—
    A headsail jumps through the thinning haze.
The whole hull follows, till—broad around us—
    The clean-swept ocean says: "Go your ways!"

MORNING MIST
S. C. W. 1928

Bound for Blue Water–1

We're bound for blue water where the great winds blow,
It's time to get the tacks aboard, time for us to go;
The crowd's at the capstan and the tune's in the shout,
"A long pull, a strong pull, and warp the hooker out."

The bow-wash is eddying, spreading from the bows,
Aloft and loose the topsails and some one give a rouse;
A salt Atlantic chanty shall be music to the dead,
"A long pull, a strong pull, and the yard to the masthead."

Bound for
Blue Water – II

Green and merry run the seas, the wind comes cold,
Salt and strong and pleasant, and worth a mint of gold;
And she's staggering, swooping, as she feels her feet,
"A long pull, a strong pull, and aft the main-sheet."

Shrilly squeal the running sheaves, the weather-gear strains,
Such a clatter of chain-sheets, the devil's in the chains;
Over us the bright stars, under us the drowned,
"A long pull, a strong pull, and we're outward bound!"

Yonder, round and ruddy, is the mellow old moon,
The red-funneled tug has gone, and now, sonny, soon
We'll be clear of the channel, so watch how you steer,
"Ease her when she pitches, and so-long, my dear!"

Karlssen's Yarn

"I was in a hooker once," said Karlssen,
"And Bill, as was a seaman, died,
So we lashed him in an old tarpaulin
And tumbled him across the side;
And the fun of it was that all his gear was
Divided up among the crew
Before that blushing human error,
Our crawling little captain, knew.

"On the passage home one morning
(As certain as I prays for grace)
There was old Bill's shadder a-hauling
At the weather mizzen-topsail brace.
He was all grown green with sea-weed,
He was all lashed up and shored;
So I says to him, I says, 'Why, Billy!
What's a-bringin' of you back aboard?'

"'I'm a-weary of them there mermaids,'
Says old Bill's ghost to me;
'It ain't no place for a Christian
Below there—under sea.
For it's all blown sand and shipwrecks,
And old bones eaten bare,
And them cold fishy females
With long green weeds for hair.

"'And there ain't no dances shuffled,
And no old yarns is spun,
And there ain't no stars but starfish,
And never any moon or sun.
I heard your keel a-passing
And the running rattle of the brace,'
And he says, 'Stand by,' says William,
'For a shift towards a better place.'

"Well, he sogered about decks till sunrise,
When a rooster in the hen-coop crowed,
And as so much smoke he faded
And as so much smoke he goed;
And I've often wondered since, Jan,
How his old ghost stands to fare
Long o' them cold fishy females
With long green weeds for hair!"

Crossing the Line

We were then in about five degrees of North Latitude, the trades had failed us, and the doldrums claimed their share of bracing and hauling, giving us little time for any other work. Every ripple on the brazen sea called for a different angle of the yards, and in dead calm we lay with our head yards braced sharp up and the after yards square, the courses guyed out from the masts by slap lines and bowlines. During the day a vertical sun beat down on our bare deck in unmerciful fashion, lifting the scorching pitch from the seams and all but addling our senses with the heat. The mates became more and more exacting, every job palled, and the stuffy, unpalatable food of the fo'c'sle stuck in our throats. The vessel was a chip of hell floating on the unforgiving ocean; riveted for days, that stretched to weeks, amid the patches of rusty sea weed, a thousand feet across, that tangled about the rudder post, great sun-scorched fragments of the dead Sargasso Sea.

And all of this time we knew that the Southern branch of the Equatorial Current was sending us back to the W. N. W. at the rate of several miles a day!

In watch below, choking with the heat, we lay tossing sleeplessly in our bunks while the sickly smell of the bilges came up from the fore peak through the wind sails let down to ventilate the hold. Cockroaches throve in added millions, and we were treated to our first rations of weevily tack. The little white worms seemed to be everywhere. The cracker hash was riddled with them as Chow selected the rottenest bread for this purpose. Most of us developed boils, and the dark brown taste, left by the vile food, resulted in a general loss of appetite. The heat even forced the rats from the hold and on a dark night we could hear them scampering about under the fo'c'sle head. The healthy sea tan of the temperate zone left our faces, and we became peevish and morose.

· · ·

About this time considerable activity went on forward among the old sailors in both watches. One dog watch, men from both sides of the fo'c'sle went aft and interviewed the captain.

"We are near the line," said Frenchy to me shortly afterward. "Don't make any fuss about what goes on, and you'll get off easy," he cautioned.

There were quite a few of us who had never crossed the equator, and the preparations in the dog watches augured ill for those who chose to resist the just tribute demanded by Father Neptune of all green sailors who, in those days, ventured across the magic bounds.

A fair slant of wind had helped us along for a few days, when the Old Man called Jimmy aft and imparted important information.

At eight bells in the afternoon watch, as all hands were mustering in the waist, a hoarse hail from forward greeted us.

"*Ship Ahoy! Ship Ahoy!*" came the deep bass summons from a point beneath the bow.

"Forward, there! Who hails us?" answered the captain, who stood out on the poop, replying to the voice from forward.

"Father Neptune hails us, Captain," answered Hitchen, returning from the bow. "He asks if there are any of his children on board who would receive his blessing on their heads."

"Aye, bring him on board," ordered the skipper, a broad grin lighting his features, and the two mates reflected the feeling aft by joining in the smiles.

A noise of trudging along the deck followed, the King of the Sea, his own whiskers hidden behind a broad beard of rope yarns, a bright red harpoon in his right hand serving as a trident, and a large razor, made of hoop iron, stuck in his belt, walked aft. He was draped in the folds of an old boat sail, and for all of his regal trimmings we recognized the famous Jimmy. A retinue followed, rigged out in true deep-water style, and carrying a tub between them, which was deposited on deck just aft of the mainmast.

"Captain," said Neptune, "I am told as 'ow you 'ave green 'ands on board who 'ave to be shaved."

"Yes, Your Majesty, we have some with the hayseed still in their whiskers," answered the skipper.

"Bring 'em forth!" thundered the King, unlimbering his razor and passing the trident to the safe keeping of his wife, Amphitrite, in the person of Axel, who towered two feet above the head of the King.

However, what Jimmy lacked in stature he made up in efficiency, and in the imperious glance of scorn with which he greeted eight of us who were lined up for his inspection.

Old Smith grabbed me by the neck; I was seated on the bottom of an upturned bucket at the feet of the King.

"Your name?" demanded His Majesty, and as I was about to answer a filthy swab of soapsuds and grease was thrust in my mouth and smeared over my face and the shaving began, ending by a back somersault into the tub of water behind.

"Next!" called Neptune in true barber shop style, and so, in turn, each of the green hands went through the ordeal; the least willing getting the most attention. Scouse and Joe were among the lubbers, and were accorded special rites to the vast amusement of

all hands. Australia wound up the entertainment by handing Scouse and Joe pieces of gunny sack, smeared with black paint, with which to wipe their faces.

"All right now!" called the mate, after the skipper had left the deck. "Turn to and clean up," and we were back again to the rigid discipline of the sea, relaxed for a brief hour to let King Neptune hold his sway.

Rain

There were intervals when the heavens opened and showered their blessing down on us. One day the skies darkened, and the horizon was blotted out by a wall of rain. It was a perfect deluge. We plugged all the scupper holes and in a short time the deck was flooded inches deep with delicious rain water. We all stripped to the skin and everything washable was brought out on deck, which soon resembled a busy laundry. None of us had felt fresh water on our faces, let alone our bodies, since we left Cardiff, and what a luxury a real necessity can become! Personal hygiene simply had no place on a windjammer. The downpour also served to replenish our supply of fresh water in the tank down in the hold.

And so we drifted along the doldrums, gradually edging our way south until one morning at eight bells we were called out to find the ship heeling slightly and the welcome sound of rippling waters along the bow. A breeze had sprung up during the night, and this time it was no false alarm. It carried us steadily south, leaving the doldrums behind. The light sails were unbent and replaced by storm canvas.

She Was Alive, Immortal!

We were at sea off the River Plate, running south like a stag. The wind had been slowly freshening for twenty-four hours, and for one whole day we had whitened the sea like a battleship. Our run for the day had been 271 knots, which we thought a wonderful run, though it has, of course, been exceeded by many ships. For this ship it was an exceptional run. The wind was on the quarter, her best point of sailing, and there was enough wind for a glutton. Our captain had the reputation of being a "cracker-on," and on this one occasion he drove her till she groaned. For that one wonderful day we staggered and swooped, and bounded in wild leaps, and burrowed down and shivered, and anon rose up shaking. The wind roared up aloft and boomed in the shrouds, and the sails bellied out as stiff as iron. We tore through the sea in great jumps—there is no other word for it. She seemed to leap clear from one green roaring ridge to come smashing down upon the next. I have been in a fast steamer—a very fast turbine steamer—doing more than twenty knots, but she gave me no sense of great speed. In this old sailing ship the joy of the hurry was such that we laughed and cried aloud. The noise of the wind booming, and the clack, clack, clack of the sheet-blocks, and the ridged seas roaring past us, and the groaning and whining of every block and plank, were like tunes for a dance. We seemed to be tearing through it at ninety miles an hour. Our wake whitened and broadened, and rushed away aft in a creamy fury. We were running here, and hurrying there, taking a small pull of this, and getting another inch of that, till we were weary. But as we hauled we sang and shouted. We were possessed of the spirits of the wind. We could have danced and killed each other. We were in an ecstasy. We were possessed. We half believed that the ship would leap from the waters and hurl herself into the heavens, like a winged god. Over her bows came the sprays in showers of sparkles. Her foresail was wet to the yard. Her scuppers were brooks. Her swing-ports spouted like cataracts. Recollect, too, that it was a day to make your heart glad. It was a clear day, a sunny day, a day of brightness and splendour. The sun was glorious in the sky. The sky was of a blue unspeakable. We were tearing along across a splendour of sea that made you sing. Far as one could see there was the water shining and shaking. Blue it was, and green it was, and of a dazzling brilliance in the sun. It rose up in hills and in ridges. It smashed into a foam and roared. It towered up again and toppled. It mounted and shook in a rhythm, in a tune, in a music. One could have flung one's body to it as a sacrifice. One longed to be in it, to be a part of it, to be beaten and banged by it. It was a wonder and a glory and a terror. It was a triumph, it was royal, to see that beauty.

And later, after a day of it, as we sat below, we felt our mad ship taking yet wilder leaps, bounding over yet more boisterous hollows, and shivering and exulting in every inch of her. She seemed filled with a fiery, unquiet life. She seemed inhuman, glorious, spiritual. One forgot that she was man's work. We forgot that we were men. She was alive, immortal, furious. We were her minions and servants. We were the star-dust whirled in the train of the comet. We banged our plates with the joy we had in her. We sang and shouted, and called her the glory of the seas.

Ship's Log

July 15   Lat. 41.28 Lon. 61.07 NW NW WNW Moderate & Pleasant 4 PM Saw the Land WNW 25 miles; Middle fresh & Cloudy with light Rain Squalls, Latter light breezes & cloudy with light Rain Squalls No observations

July 16   Lat. 44.23 Lon. 63.29 Calm SE NE Faint Airs & Calms, Middle & Latter fresh & baffling with cloudy weather Spoke ship Harriet Erving 79 days from Boston for Valparaiso

July 17   Lat. 47.32 Lon. 64.55 NE ESE ESE Light breezes thick weather Latter moderate No observations

July 18   Lat. 48.56 Lon. 65.30 SE ESE ESE Faint airs & drizzling Rain, 4 PM in Studding Sails, 10 hours 30 minutes Sounded 65 fathoms

July 19   Lat. 49.39 Lon. 66.17 Calm N^d N^d Mostly Calm thick weather sometimes Rain

July 20   Lat. 54.25 Lon. 65.00 ENE ENE NE Light increasing breezes from Northward & veering gradually to ENE, Winds cloudy, 3 hours 30 minutes set Lauboard Studding Sails, at 10 in studding sails, weather Rainy with sleet & Squally Mid^t in topgallant sails, at 4 AM close Reefed Topsails & furled Courses wind blowing a hard gale with thick Weather & snow, at 11 AM obliged to wave ship & haul off to Northward Cape St. Diego bearing by Estimate S 9 degrees W 16 miles, no observations.

July 21   Lat. 54.02 Lon. 65.00 NE NE SE Blowing hard with snow & Rain, at 1 AM saw a large ship standing NE with loss of Foresail

July 22   Lat. 54.41 Lon. 64.50 ESE SE by S E Hard Gale with Rain & sleet shipping much water bad sea Running, at 4 PM Weather fair Saw Cape St. Diego bearing SE 15 miles, wore ship at 5 PM to NE, at 6 AM wore ship to Southward at 10 saw the land South 20 miles, at meridian St. Diego W 10 miles Weather moderate & Cloudy

July 23   Lat. 56.04 Lon. 68.16 E E E Moderate all set sail passed through St. Le Marie & Cleared the Land at 6 PM, Strong tide setting to Northward Middle Rainy, Latter fair Cape Horn N 5 miles at 8 AM, the whole coast covered with snow—wild Ducks numerous, . . .

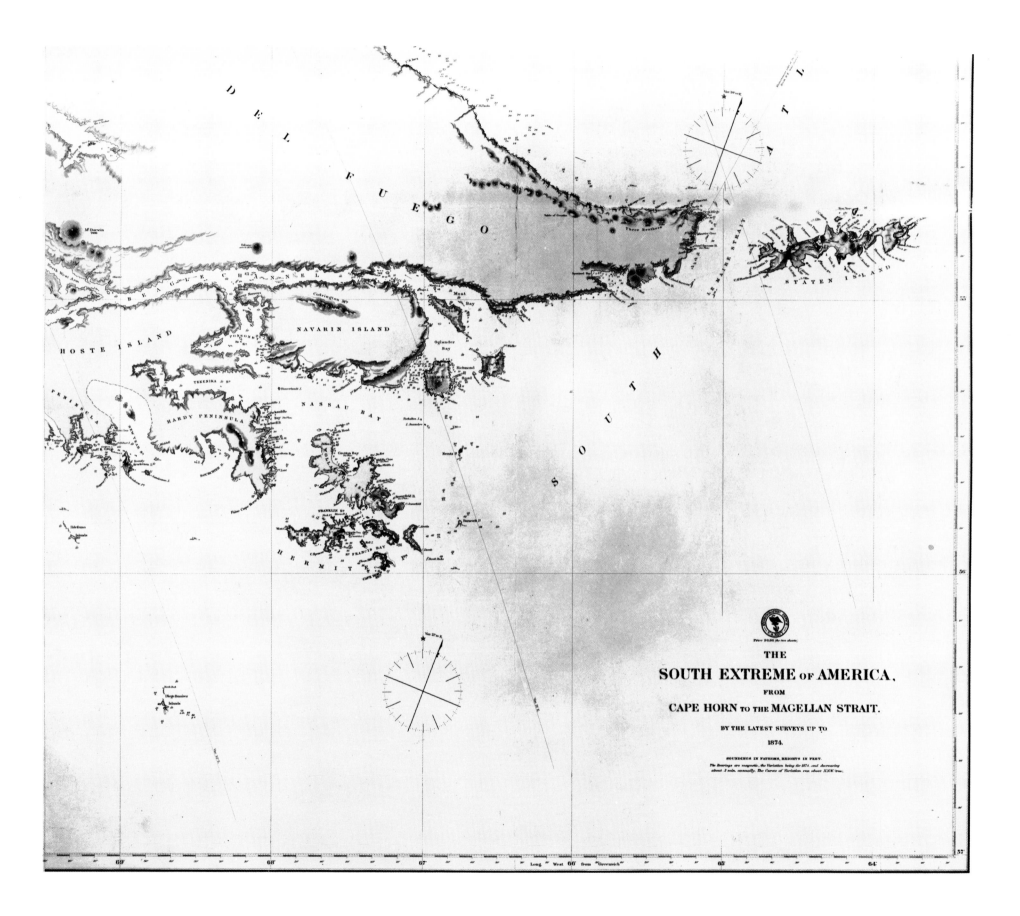

THE
SOUTH EXTREME OF AMERICA,
FROM
CAPE HORN TO THE MAGELLAN STRAIT.

BY THE LATEST SURVEYS UP TO
1874.

SOUNDINGS IN FATHOMS, HEIGHTS IN FEET.
The Bearings are magnetic, the Variation being for 1874, and decreasing
about 3 min. annually. The Curves of Variation run about NNW true.

Cape Horn Fog

All through the windless night the clipper rolled
In a great swell with oily gradual heaves
Which rolled her down until her time-bells tolled,
Clang, and the weltering water moaned like beeves.
The thundering rattle of slatting shook the sheaves,
Startles of water made the swing ports gush,
The sea was moaning and sighing and saying "Hush!"

It was all black and starless. Peering down
Into the water, trying to pierce the gloom,
One saw a dim, smooth, oily glitter of brown
Heaving and dying away and leaving room
For yet another. Like the march of doom
Came those great powers of marching silences;
Then fog came down, dead-cold, and hid the seas.

They set the Dauber to the foghorn. There
He stood upon the poop, making to sound
Out of the pump the sailor's nasal blare,
Listening lest ice should make the note resound.
She bayed there like a solitary hound
Lost in a covert; all the watch she bayed.
The fog, come closelier down, no answer made.

Denser it grew, until the ship was lost.
The elemental hid her; she was merged
In mufflings of dark death, like a man's ghost,
New to the change of death, yet thither urged.
Then from the hidden waters something surged—
Mournful, despairing, great, greater than speech,
A noise like one slow wave on a still beach.

Mournful, and then again mournful, and still
Out of the night that mighty voice arose;
The Dauber at his foghorn felt the thrill.
Who rode that desolate sea? What forms were those?
Mournful, from things defeated, in the throes
Of memory of some conquered hunting-ground,
Out of the night of death arose the sound.

"Whales!" said the Mate. They stayed there all night long
Answering the horn. Out of the night they spoke,
Defeated creatures who had suffered wrong,
But were still noble underneath the stroke.
They filled the darkness when the Dauber woke;
The men came peering to the rail to hear,
And the sea sighed, and the fog rose up sheer.

A wall of nothing at the world's last edge,
Where no life came except defeated life.
The Dauber felt shut in within a hedge,
Behind which form was hidden and thought was rife,
And that a blinding flash, a thrust, a knife
Would sweep the hedge away and make all plain,
Brilliant beyond all words, blinding the brain.

So the night passed, but then no morning broke—
Only a something showed that night was dead.
A sea-bird, cackling like a devil, spoke,
And the fog drew away and hung like lead.
Like mighty cliffs it shaped, sullen and red;
Like glowering gods at watch it did appear,
And sometimes drew away, and then drew near.

Like islands, and like chasms, and like hell,
But always mighty and red, gloomy and ruddy,
Shutting the visible sea in like a well;
Slow heaving in vast ripples, blank and muddy,
Where the sun should have risen it streaked bloody.
The day was still-born; all the sea-fowl scattering
Splashed the still water, mewing, hovering, clattering.

Polar Snow

Then Polar snow came down little and light,
Till all the sky was hidden by the small,
Most multitudinous drift of dirty white
Tumbling and wavering down and covering all—
Covering the sky, the sea, the clipper tall,
Furring the ropes with white, casing the mast,
Coming on no known air, but blowing past.

And all the air seemed full of gradual moan,
As though in those cloud-chasms the horns were blowing
The mort for gods cast out and overthrown,
Or for the eyeless sun plucked out and going.
Slow the low gradual moan came in the snowing;
The Dauber felt the prelude had begun.
The snowstorm fluttered by; he saw the sun

Show and pass by, gleam from one towering prison
Into another, vaster and more grim,
Which in dull crags of darkness had arisen
To muffle-to a final door on him.
The gods upon the dull crags lowered dim,
The pigeons chattered, quarrelling in the track.
In the south-west the dimness dulled to black.

All Hands on Deck!

Then came the cry of "Call all hands on deck!"
The Dauber knew its meaning; it was come:
Cape Horn, that tramples beauty into wreck,
And crumples steel and smites the strong man dumb.
Down clattered flying kites and staysails: some
Sang out in quick, high calls: the fair-leads skirled,
And from the south-west came the end of the world.

"Caught in her ball-dress," said the Bosun, hauling;
"Lee-ay, lee-ay!" quick, high, come the men's call;
It was all wallop of sails and startled calling.
"Let fly!" "Let go!" "Clew up!" and "Let go all!"
"Now up and make them fast!" "Here, give us a haul!"
"Now up and stow them! Quick! By God! we're done!"
The blackness crunched all memory of the sun.

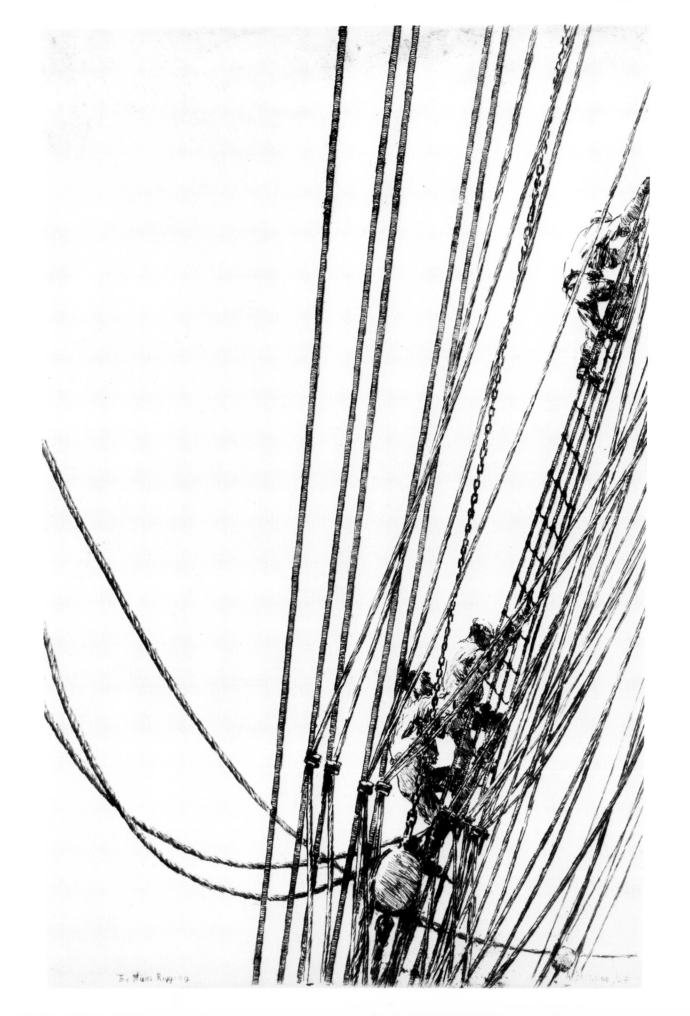

Fr. Main Rigging

Up, Damn You!

"Up!" said the Mate. "Mizen top-gallants. Hurry!"
The Dauber ran, the others ran, the sails
Slatted and shook; out of the black a flurry
Whirled in fine lines, tattering the edge to trails.
Painting and art and England were old tales
Told in some other life to that pale man,
Who struggled with white fear and gulped and ran.

He struck a ringbolt in his haste and fell—
Rose, sick with pain, half-lamed in his left knee;
He reached the shrouds where clambering men pell-mell
Hustled each other up and cursed him; he
Hurried aloft with them: then from the sea
Came a cold, sudden breath that made the hair
Stiff on the neck, as though Death whispered there.

A man below him punched him in the side.
"Get up, you Dauber, or let me get past."
He saw the belly of the skysail skied,
Gulped, and clutched tight, and tried to go more fast.
Sometimes he missed his ratline and was grassed,
Scraped his shin raw against the rigid line
The clamberers reached the futtock-shrouds' incline.

Cursing they came; one, kicking out behind,
Kicked Dauber in the mouth, and one below
Punched at his calves; the futtock-shrouds inclined
It was a perilous path for one to go.
"Up, Dauber, up!" A curse followed a blow.
He reached the top and gasped, then on, then on.
And one voice yelled "Let go!" and one "All gone!"

Fierce clamberers, some in oilskins, some in rags,
Hustling and hurrying up, up the steep stairs.
Before the windless sails were blown to flags,
And whirled like dirty birds athwart great airs,
Ten men in all, to get this mast of theirs
Snugged to the gale in time. "Up! Damn you, run!"
The mizen topmast head was safely won.

Lay Out

"Lay out!" the Bosun yelled. The Dauber laid
Out on the yard, gripping the yard and feeling
Sick at the mighty space of air displayed
Below his feet, where mewing birds were wheeling.
A giddy fear was on him; he was reeling.
He bit his lip half through, clutching the jack.
A cold sweat glued the shirt upon his back.

The yard was shaking, for a brace was loose.
He felt that he would fall; he clutched, he bent,
Clammy with natural terror to the shoes
While idiotic promptings came and went.
Snow fluttered on a wind-flaw and was spent;
He saw the water darken. Someone yelled,
"Frap it; don't stay to furl! Hold on!" He held.

Blown to Rags

How long the gale had blown he could not tell,
Only the world had changed, his life had died.
A moment now was everlasting hell.
Nature an onslaught from the weather side,
A withering rush of death, a frost that cried,
Shrieked, till he withered at the heart; a hail
Plastered his oilskins with an icy mail.

"Cut!" yelled his mate. He looked—the sail was gone,
Blown into rags in the first furious squall;
The tatters drummed the devil's tattoo. On
The buckling yard a block thumped like a mall.
The ship lay—the sea smote her, the wind's bawl
Came, "loo, loo, loo!" The devil cried his hounds
On to the poor spent stag strayed in his bounds.

"Cut! Ease her!" yelled his mate; the Dauber heard.
His mate wormed up the tilted yard and slashed,
A rag of canvas skimmed like a darting bird.
The snow whirled, the ship bowed to it, the gear lashed,
The sea-tops were cut off and flung down smashed;
Tatters of shouts were flung, the rags of yells—
And clang, clang, clang, below beat the two bells.

"O God!" the Dauber moaned. A roaring rang,
Blasting the royals like a cannonade;
The backstays parted with a crackling clang,
The upper spars were snapped like twigs decayed—
Snapped at their heels, their jagged splinters splayed,
Like white and ghastly hairs erect with fear.
The Mate yelled, "Gone, by God, and pitched them clear!"

"Up!" yelled the Bosun; "up and clear the wreck!"
The Dauber followed where he led: below
He caught one giddy glimpsing of the deck
Filled with white water, as though heaped with snow.
He saw the streamers of the rigging blow
Straight out like pennons from the splintered mast,
Then, all sense dimmed, all was an icy blast

Roaring from nether hell and filled with ice,
Roaring and crashing on the jerking stage,
An utter bridle given to utter vice,
Limitless power mad with endless rage
Withering the soul; a minute seemed an age.
He clutched and hacked at ropes, at rags of sail
Thinking that comfort was a fairy-tale

Told long ago—long, long ago—long since
Heard of in other lives—imagined, dreamed—
There where the basest beggar was a prince
To him in torment where the tempest screamed,
Comfort and warmth and ease no longer seemed
Things that a man could know: soul, body, brain,
Knew nothing but the wind, the cold, the pain.

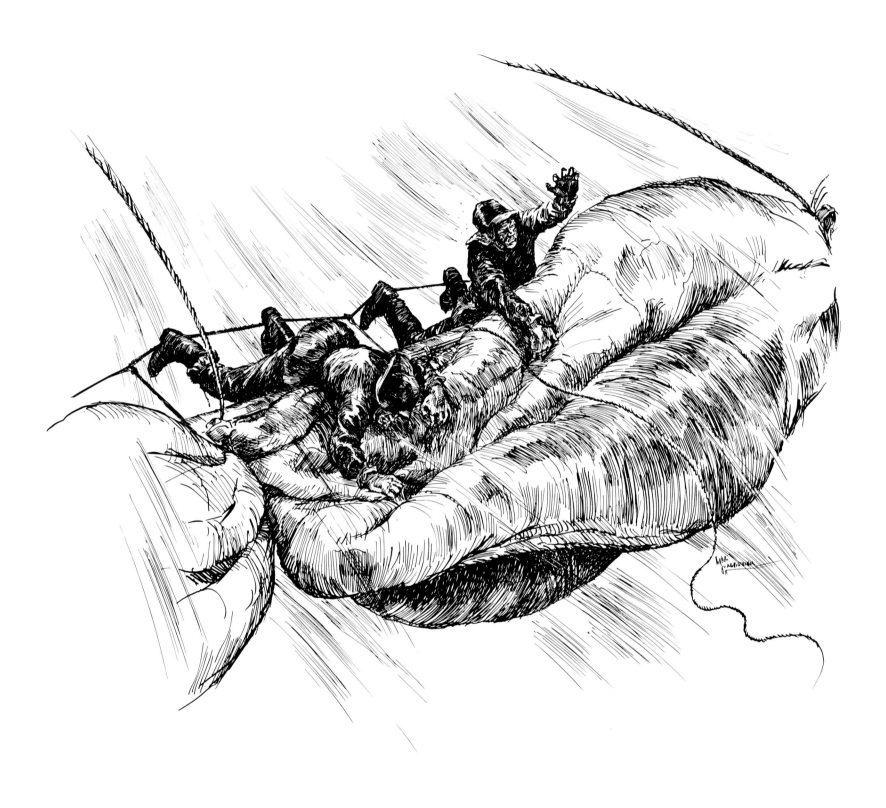

Growl You May, But Go You Must

"Leave that!" the Bosun shouted; "Crojick save!"
The splitting crojick, not yet gone to rags,
Thundered below, beating till something gave,
Bellying between its buntlines into bags.
Some birds were blown past, shrieking: dark, like shags,
Their backs seemed, looking down. "Leu, leu!" they cried.
The ship lay, the seas thumped her; she had died.

They reached the crojick yard, which buckled, buckled
Like a thin whalebone to the topsail's strain.
They laid upon the yard and heaved and knuckled,
Pounding the sail, which jangled and leapt again.
It was quite hard with ice, its rope like chain,
Its strength like seven devils; it shook the mast.
They cursed and toiled and froze: a long time passed.

Two hours passed, then a dim lightening came.
Those frozen ones upon the yard could see
The mainsail and the foresail still the same,
Still battling with the hands and blowing free,
Rags tattered where the staysails used to be.
The lower topsails stood; the ship's lee deck
Seethed with four feet of water filled with wreck.

An hour more went by; the Dauber lost
All sense of hands and feet, all sense of all
But of a wind that cut him to the ghost,
And of a frozen fold he had to haul,
Of heavens that fell and never ceased to fall,
And ran in smoky snatches along the sea,
Leaping from crest to wave-crest, yelling. He

Lost sense of time; no bells went, but he felt
Ages go over him. At last, at last
They frapped the cringled crojick's icy pelt;
In frozen bulge and bunt they made it fast.
Then, scarcely live, they laid in to the mast.
The Captain's speaking trumpet gave a blare,
"Make fast the topsail, Mister, while you're there."

Some seamen cursed, but up they had to go—
Up to the topsail yard to spend an hour
Stowing a topsail in a blinding snow,
Which made the strongest man among them cower.
More men came up, the fresh hands gave them power,
They stowed the sail; then with a rattle of chain
One half the crojick burst its bonds again.

The Ninth Great Wave

They stowed the sail, frapping it round with rope,
Leaving no surface for the wind, no fold,
Then down the weather shrouds, half dead, they grope;
That struggle with the sail had made them old.
They wondered if the crojick furl would hold.
"Lucky," said one, "it didn't spring the spar."
"Lucky!" the Bosun said, "Lucky! We are!"

She came within two shakes of turning top
Or stripping all her shroud-screws, that first quiff.
"Now fish those wash-deck buckets out of the slop.
Here's Dauber says he doesn't like Cape Stiff.
This isn't wind, man, this is only a whiff.
Hold on, all hands, hold on!" a sea, half seen,
Paused, mounted, burst, and filled the main-deck green.

The Dauber felt a mountain of water fall.
It covered him deep, deep, he felt it fill,
Over his head, the deck, the fife-rails, all,
Quieting the ship, she trembled and lay still.
Then with a rush and shatter and clanging shrill
Over she went; he saw the water cream
Over the bitts; he saw the half-deck stream.

Then in the rush he swirled, over she went;
Her lee-rail dipped, he struck, and something gave;
His legs went through a port as the roll spent;
She paused, then rolled, and back the water drave.
He drifted with it as a part of the wave,
Drowning, half-stunned, exhausted, partly frozen,
He struck the booby hatchway; then the Bosun

Leaped, seeing his chance, before the next sea burst,
And caught him as he drifted, seized him, held,
Up-ended him against the bitts, and cursed.
"This ain't the George's Swimming Baths," he yelled;
"Keep on your feet!" Another grey-back felled
The two together, and the Bose, half-blind,
Spat: "One's a joke," he cursed, "but two's unkind."

"Now, damn it, Dauber!" said the Mate. "Look out,
Or you'll be over the side!"

Coiling Down

The water freed;
Each clanging freeing-port became a spout.
The men cleared up the decks as there was need.
The Dauber's head was cut, he felt it bleed
Into his oilskins as he clutched and coiled.
Water and sky were devil's brews which boiled,

Boiled, shrieked, and glowered; but the ship was saved.
Snugged safely down, though fourteen sails were split.
Out of the dark a fiercer fury raved.
The grey-backs died and mounted, each crest lit
With a white toppling gleam that hissed from it
And slid, or leaped, or ran with whirls of cloud,
Mad with inhuman life that shrieked aloud.

The watch was called; Dauber might go below.
"Splice the main brace!" the Mate called. All laid aft
To get a gulp of momentary glow
As some reward for having saved the craft.
The steward ladled mugs, from which each quaff'd
Whisky, with water, sugar, and lime-juice, hot,
A quarter of a pint each made the tot.

Beside the lamp-room door the steward stood
Ladling it out, and each man came in turn,
Tipped his sou'-wester, drank it, grunted "Good!"
And shambled forward, letting it slowly burn. . . .

Cape Horn Rescue-1

"Sail ho!"

"Ay, ay!" shouted back Sayle, the second mate. "Where away is she showing?"

"Two points on the stabbud bow!"

Evidently Sayle had altered helm, for the patch of solid matter had swung right ahead. It was Captain Fegan who next roared: "How's she bear now, topsail yard, there?"

"Right ahead, sir!"

I heard Sayle's voice: "He's showing bunting, sir!"

Very forlorn and untidy she showed. When she rolled—soddenly, with no suggestion of that strange liveliness which distinguishes a *fighting* ship—she showed her hull clear to the keel.

"She's the *Minotaur*, sir!"

The *Minotaur* was a far nobler ship than the *Dovenby*. She had been something of a clipper in her heyday, built especially for the wool-run from Melbourne home. And now—now she was a wreck; and the bunting Sayle had reported was the Red Ensign, tattered, flying Union-down. That is a signal of distress known the wide world over. Very different she appeared from the trim, graceful beauty of so few weeks before. Then she was proud and triumphant, "walking the waters like a thing of life"; now she was disheveled, pitiful. The heart had gone out of her. Not a stitch of canvas remained. She slugged wearily to the boisterous compulsion of the greedy waves.

Sea after sea surged over her, but, as evidence of the fighting spirit of her crew, each time she shook herself free of that devastating water, figures, diminished into the likeness of ants by distance, showed at the foot of the mainmast, and I knew the men were pumping hard, determined to continue the struggle until the final roller swamped them under and gave them such peace as the windjammer sailor usually earned.

The *Minotaur*'s cargo had shifted in the furious weather she had met off Diego Ramirez. A succession of giant seas had stove in the main hatch. Naturally, the intruding water went to the low side and increased the heel, as she wallowed, semi-defenceless.

Cape Horn Rescue–II

Taking off a distressed crew of twenty-five men could not be done casually.

Fegan was shrewd. To jockey into position to wind'ard of the *Minotaur*, drift down as near as safety permitted, and so lessen the wet road to be taken by the boat, was his aim. He took in all square sail—going aloft to do that warmed our frozen bodies—and kept her under lower stay-sails, since speed or comfort were no longer main desiderata.

There was no melodramatic appeal for volunteers. Mr. Perkins simply turned about from overseeing the readying of the lee lifeboat and barked:

"Which of you's coming, then? You, Jeffreys?" Jeffreys began to strip off his oilskins and kick off his seaboots. That was answer enough. He didn't intend to be hampered by weighty clothing if he ended up in the sea. Chamberlain and Elliott followed his example; so did Rhys and then—not so briskly—Macauley.

"I want five men," said the mate, "and a boy for the bow." The boy was to be ready to leap up a rope and effect communication with the floundering *Minotaur* in case her own people were too frozen to aid themselves. Someone nimble and agile, fairly muscular. I was all three.

"You like to try it, Shaw?" snarled the mate, as if sentencing me to death, not asking my collaboration in a forlorn hope.

When Fegan was satisfied that the ship was in position he threw her into the wind; her fore-and-aft canvas slatted frantically as all way was checked.

"Watch your chance, mister!" he trumpeted. "Good luck!"

"Ay, ay, sir," grunted Perkins. "Take the weight on your capstans!" Sayle was in charge of the heaving out; Fegan took control of the lowering. The capstans clanked; as the boat lifted its keel from the chocks the ship shuddered, leaned viciously to wind'ard, and then took in half the Cape Horn sea. It seemed no less. The men at the capstans were hurled into the scuppers. The boat settled back into the chocks. At the next attempt, the boat was lifted and swung out. Then it became a furious fight to save her from being stove against the side. We who had jumped in had all our work to keep her fended off, with stretcher, boat-hook, oar-loom. The lifeboat was lifted high above the rail, then fell into roaring vortices. Only most Herculean efforts saved it from being smashed small. But it was clear.

Cape Horn Rescue–III

As soon as we emerged from the ship's shelter the weight of wind sent us along, and Mr. Perkins ordered a reefed sail to be set! That was a feat of no common cleverness. But this ex-North Sea cabin-boy could have sailed a scow round the world, I think. We got up the diminished sail, and the boat plunged ahead, tearing the waves to foam and froth. Occasionally a high wave towered as if about to swamp us; and had a weak man been at the steering oar—Perkins disdained the rudder, which the seas might easily unhook from its pintles—we must have broached to and been overwhelmed. But we ran away from each comber as it curled and crashed; our wake was a maelstrom; a high wave towered beside each bow.

Actually, the time taken in crossing from ship to ship was too short to allow any noticeable emotions to grow. I bailed furiously when ordered to do so. Exposed there in the boat the cold was indescribable—ice clogged my jersey, my bootless feet were like frozen marble. We wore no lifebelts.

Whilst we were crossing that half-mile or so of ugly water—soaring high to see the wreck ahead, swooping deeply until it felt as if we could never lift again, with spindrift slashing everywhere, and the boat itself appearing to spin in giddy circles—Captain Fegan—crafty seaman!—got the *Dovenby* under way again and, as soon as we saw we were clear of such scant shelter as the low hull afforded, worked the barque down to leeward of the *Minotaur*. This in itself, with a harassed ship, was no trifling feat of seamanship, especially considering how shorthanded he was with almost half his crew away in the lifeboat. But he knew that for the boat to attempt to return against wind and sea was an impossibility; whereas, down to leeward of the wreck, we might stand a fighting chance. So, using his skill and definite courage, he took the roaring fabric across the wreck's stern, and wore her round on her other side. It meant loosening canvas, setting it, and furling it again—everything there being ice-bound; but he did it. In all the bright lexicon of windjamming there was no such word as "fail"!

Meantime, we threshed on, until Mr. Perkins deemed it well to douse the sail and rely on oars. The boat almost capsized at that juncture.

We got the boat within close hail of the hard-set *Minotaur*. Mr. Perkins was railing at the crew now they were pulling hard. He used language that might have set the sodden timbers on fire. Had he employed similar words on the *Dovenby*'s decks he would probably have been brained with a belaying-pin; but no one cared; indeed, his savage ferocity of word and act was afterwards praised by us as showing the caliber of hard-case man he was!

I lent my weight to the bow oar. It seemed trivial help. Over my shoulder I saw the wreck at close quarters; she looked squalid and pitiful and the havoc wrought in her by the processional waves was very evident. Even when lifted by the seas she was sodden, and when she sank back it appeared as if she would never climb to open air again. So clean-swept was she that every man of her crew had taken refuge in the rigging; the captain was lowermost. Her deckhouses were torn open—we used to admire them, for they were built of teakwood and rather ornately carved. Her poop-break had once been a picture of bright wood and brass. But a loose spar had carried along the swilling decks and its heel had served as a battering-ram to hammer in that trickery; the cabin windows were empty holes out of which water sluiced as she dived. Desolation made manifest is the impression I still retain of her.

To approach her from the weather side must have been fatal—any wave might have swung the boat against the hull and bilged it irremediably. Mr. Perkins was not a tyro—he steered for us to pass under the squattering stern. To leeward was a considerable tangle of wreckage. Although the masts were cut away the action of the sea had kept them close alongside; a rope was fouled to serve as painter—a wire rope that could not be cut. The spars pounded the hull. It was not easy to discover a passage in the curdled debris through which the boat could approach with safety to herself; but sea-wise Perkins discovered it. I have a vague impression of fending off loose wreckage with a boathook, then of clawing a hold into the chains. I remember the *Minotaur*'s captain yelling: "Hurry—hurry—she's all but gone!"

Cape Horn Rescue–IV

Jeffreys was sent to join me in the bow—to fend off as I received our salvage, which came down, man by man, the first one grasping our painter and taking a hitch with it. Just as he slithered down the rope—he was frozen so that he could hardly move—the painter tore apart. He went overside; I grabbed him; got an arm, hooked his hand over our gunwale, then fetched him in like a sack of coals. His face was piteously blue, but his stiff lips said: "Thanks, mate!" He was pushed underfoot; we took in the next one.

It was a wild, senseless scrabble, actually. Details do not stand out clearly; everything was so breathless and so intensely cold and uncomfortable. I felt as if my arms were dragged from their sockets a score of times. I was hit, kicked in the face by the boots of men coming down the line that was thrown to replace our broken painter. I remember reaching over to grab one man who'd jumped at the wrong moment and missed the mark—the suction alongside was dragging him under; I had a hold of his pants-seat and a wrinkle of his shirt, and I swore I'd hang on till hell froze over! Jeffreys spared a hand just as I was being dragged over to join him;

his bull-like strength swung him in, the lurch of the boat aiding human effort; and the man's fingernails raked down my face from temple to chin. I didn't feel the pain until much later, when I thawed out!

"Look alive!" Perkins was braying ceaselessly, as he worked his oar like a scull to keep the bow close in, since it was now not possible to use the pulling oars, because of the loose wreckage on which they might break—and we had no spares.

One of the *Minotaur*'s men lost his hold of the rope as he slithered down and he fell between boat and ship's side. A wave pyramided over him, and there was a fragment of timber in its foamy crest; it hurled itself at the submerged man and sank him—I saw a thin tinge of red appear in the curdled water, nothing more.

But when another missed the boat—a slim boy—and fell into the sea, to reappear on the other side, having passed clean under the keel—Rhys, elderly, rheumatic as he was, owner of a weak heart, jumped over the side after him and grasped him, hanging to the gunwale with one tattooed hand and the boy with the other, until Chamberlain and Macauley got their hands under his armpits and brought him back.

When 14 people had come thus, Mr. Perkins funneled his hands to hail the *Minotaur*'s captain.

"Full load—we'll be back!" he yelled undramatically.

Cape Horn Rescue–v

The captain waved his hand stiffly, but he gave us a one-man cheer. So we cast off, backed out—experiencing much the same harassment as when first leaving the *Dovenby*'s side—and settled for the return voyage. It was impossible to step the mast or set even a rag of sail; but such of the salved as could move insisted on double-banking the oars; and we slugged along toward our ship—jockeying wildly in her new position.

Once we reached the *Dovenby*'s stern, drawing in very closely, Captain Fegan hove a weighted heaving-line which fell across the boat and, when hauled in, we found a stout four-inch rope made fast to it. This simplified matters a good deal: the inboard bight of the rope was led to a capstan, and with the crew heaving staunchly we were dragged alongside. Thus all our boat's crew were free to fend off and hold on when we actually came alongside. Perkins yelled that we'd have to make a return trip.

Fegan replied—through a speaking-trumpet, the first time I'd ever known him to use one—that the weather was worsening. Meanwhile, the crew aboard the ship had pitched down bowlines and a jumping-ladder; and we were already passing up the castaways. It was quite as formidable a task as salving them—even more so, in some respects. When the ropes were thrown down they spanked us cruelly; so the entire proceeding was a blasphemous affair enough. One of our rescued broke an arm, for the boat surged away just as those above took the weight on a rope; the unfortunate man swung against the *Dovenby*'s plates and through the din we heard the bone crack—it was like a tree-branch going. Later on Captain Fegan and the *Minotaur*'s captain amputated that broken arm.

With our boat emptied of its first load, Perkins—suddenly human, for all the time of the double crossing he'd been a very devil of spluttering spite and foul-mouthedness—sang out: "Anyone want a relief? We're trying again!" The boat-crew were blown, weary; they'd seen for themselves what boatwork in that kind of sea really was; but every man refused to allow himself to be replaced.

"All right—you've done not so badly!" said Perkins; and that was the only word of commendation I ever heard from him. Next day he was as rigorous in his attitude as ever—cursing us for a lot of useless scrimshankers! The sea doesn't believe in handing out fragrant bouquets!

But Fegan passed down a bottle of diluted rum, and we all took a heartening swig, feeling we'd earned it. Then we bailed out the boat and it was hooked on to the davit-falls; these were led to the capstans and we were hove clear of the water, for the *Dovenby* had again to be jockeyed into position to wind'ard of the squattering *Minotaur*.

Cape Horn Rescue—VI

With the *Dovenby* worked back to wind'ard, the rescue work was resumed. I think we ran the boat down to the *Minotaur* in better shape the second time than the first as we were growing experienced. Moreover, we had licked the worst sea and wind could do, and we felt we could do it again. We had become a working team. Each man knew what was expected; and we were elated at having won a part-victory.

Not that this second trip was any child's play. The wind was increasing in riotous squalls that planed off the wave-crests and hurled them in milky wantonness all over the troughs and wave-flanks. But the boat was not so lively; she wasted less of her effort in swinging up and down from crest to trough; when a fierce squall caught the rag of canvas we carried—for Perkins had again heroically set sail—it sent us hurling forward like a racing yacht. Thus, in what seemed to be no time at all, we were again under the distressed ship's lee, and busy at our task of bringing hope to the well-nigh hopeless.

The intervening hours had distressed such as remained still more. They were like ice-men, lashed in the rigging, with enormous icicles depending from their feet. Indeed, since not even the captain made a move to save himself, I was ordered to get aboard and lend a hand. That was not difficult—the ship floated very low. It meant watching the exact moment for a leap; but I jumped, and found myself clawing at the chain-plates, and a wave kindly licked me higher so that I fell over the rail in a foaming bath.

The knots of the unfortunate men's lashings had frozen so stiff that their numbed fingers refused to loosen them; that was the real reason for their inertness. When my indifferent knife sawed through a lashing the victim soon recovered enough to help himself, even to offer to help me.

Thus man after man was cast loose and washed to the point where the boat waited. The scene on the *Minotaur*'s decks was awe-inspiring and pitiful, with whole water washing through the deck-houses, the galley and the fife-rails. Her soul had departed from her. I had learnt the "feel" of a ship—elastic, lively, even when in port; a springy easiness in her decks, and a suggestion of vigor, latent but present, everywhere. This was all gone from the *Minotaur*. She no longer parried the descending cataracts; she bowed her head meekly to accept these final, cruel buffets which seemed to express the sheer lack of chivalry on the sea's part. She deserved easement, she got only more furious onslaughts. But we saved the living elements of her—except for one unfortunate, who, when cut loose from the mizen-shrouds, simply slithered down them and vanished, going overboard like a shrouded corpse. The captain told us he thought he had died some while since—an elderly man, diseased, weakened by excesses, a drunken man, whose powers of resistance were exhausted.

Apart from him and the man who slipped between boat and ship, the *Dovenby*'s boat, under the splendid leadership of Mr. Perkins, saved the entire crew. And when the captain was landed on our deck and ushered below by the steward, to find hot grog and warmed blankets awaiting him, he took from his breast the ship's cat—gaunt, wringing wet, but still very much alive.

"You won't believe this," he told us on the *Dovenby* after he was rescued, "but just at dawn this morning I saw we were a goner; so I called the crew aft, gave them the biggest swig of rum they'd ever tasted—no good letting that go to the bottom—and then called them to prayers. I'm not a religious man, as you've maybe noticed; but—an hour after the men went back to the pumps, you turned up! Put that in your pipes and smoke it, next time you hear a man scoffing at the Almighty!"

D.C. Stinger

Song for All Seas, All Ships

Today a rude brief recitative,
Of ships sailing the seas, each with its special flag or ship signal,
Of unnamed heroes in the ships—of waves spreading and
    spreading far as the eye can reach,
Of dashing spray, and the winds piping and blowing,
And out of these a chant for the sailors of all nations
Fitful, like a surge

Of sea-captains young or old, and the mates, and of all intrepid sailors,
Of the few, very choice, taciturn, whom fate can never
    surprise or death dismay,
Pick'd sparingly without noise by thee old ocean, chosen by thee,
Thou sea that pickest and cullest the race in time, and unitest nations,
Suckled by thee, old husky nurse, embodying thee,
Indomitable, untamed as thee.

(Ever the heroes on water or on land, by ones or twos appearing,
Ever the stock preserv'd and never lost, though rare enough
    for seed preserv'd).

Sails

Hails from Wales,
Does Sails.

For any old thing you like to choose
From a new main course to a pair of shoes,
Or a bolt o' canvas to roll your bones
In when you voyage to Davy Jones,
Or thundering cuffers as ever you heard,
Sails is the man, you take my word!

He sits on the hatch, when it's sunny and calm,
With his specs on his nose, and his needle and palm,
Stitches and patches and yarns away
Of the ships that he knew in a bygone day,
The single topsails that once he made
For the Fiery Cross *in the China trade,*
Ringtails, watersails, Lord knows what
Old kites whose fashion near forgot.
And many a wonderful tale he tells
Of pirate junks off the Paracels,
And the great sea serpent he once saw rolled
Asleep on the water, fold on fold,
And a craft they spoke, of an unknown rig,
Beamy and bluff as a Geordie brig,
Tearing along in the teeth of the gale,
South o' the Cape, under all plain sail,
With a bloke that stood at the wheel and steered
In old-style togs, with a long white beard,
And the eyes of him, look you, burning bright,
Like coals of fire or a ship's portlight:
And "Look you, sonnies," says Sails, "I reckon
That hooker's skipper wass—Vanderdecken!"

Rolling Stone

I ain't a-goin' to sign in this ship, sonny,
    Nor sail in 'er no more:
I'm goin' to mosey round an' spend my money
    An' 'ave my run ashore,
An' then look for a ship that's bound somewheres
    as I've never been afore.

It ain't as I've got anythink agin 'er
    Of any sort or kind,
It ain't as I 'aven't 'ad as good times in 'er
    As any I can mind;
It ain't as I 'aven't 'ad as good shipmates
    as a man 'ud wish to find.

It's just that I'm fed up with things an' places,
    An' all the blessed show,
An' what I want's a fresh lot o' chaps' faces
    An' a ship as I don't know,
An' different grub an' a strange berth to lie in
    an' somewheres else to go.

I've always been that way since I was a nipper
    An' 'ooked it off to sea,
Or I daresay by now I'd 'a' been a skipper,
    Or mate at least maybe,
But if I could I wouldn't do no different
    (which I couldn't, bein' me!)

An' I ain't a-goin' to sign again, sonny,
    In this old ship no more:
I'm goin' to mosey round an' spend my money
    And 'ave my run ashore,
An' then I'll look for a ship that's goin' somewheres
    as I 'aven't been afore. . . .

GORDON GRANT / HERMAN MELVILLE

The Ship's Cook

Like most South Seamen, the *Julia*'s "caboose," or cook-house, was planted on the larboard side of the forecastle. Under such a press of canvas, and with the heavy sea running, the barque, diving her bows under, now and then shipped green glassy waves, which, breaking over the head-rails, fairly deluged that part of the ship, and washed clean aft. The caboose-house—thought to be fairly lashed down to its place—served as a sort of breakwater to the inundation.

About these times, Baltimore always wore what he called his "gale-suit," among other things comprising a Sou'-wester and a huge pair of well-anointed sea-boots, reaching almost to his knees. Thus equipped for a ducking or a drowning, as the case might be, our culinary high-priest drew to the slides of his temple, and performed his sooty rites in secret.

So afraid was the old man of being washed overboard that he actually fastened one end of a small line to his waistbands, and coiling the rest about him, made use of it as occasion required. When engaged outside, he unwound the cord, and secured one end to a ring-bolt in the deck; so that if a chance sea washed him off his feet, it could do nothing more.

One evening just as he was getting supper, the *Julia* reared up on her stern like a vicious colt, and when she settled again forward, fairly *dished* a tremendous sea. Nothing could withstand it. One side of the rotten head-bulwarks came in with a crash; it smote the caboose, tore it from its moorings, and after boxing it about, dashed it against the windlass, where it stranded. The water then poured along the deck like a flood rolling over and over, pots, pans, and kettles, and even old Baltimore himself, who went breaching along like a porpoise.

Striking the taffrail, the wave subsided, and washing from side to side, left the drowning cook high and dry on the after-hatch: his extinguished pipe still between his teeth, and almost bitten in two.

The few men on deck having sprung into the main-rigging, sailor-like, did nothing but roar at his calamity.

JOHN P. BENSON, GORDON GRANT / JOHN ROSS BROWNE

The Lookout

October 13th—"There she blows!" was sung out from the mast-head.

"Where away?" demanded the captain.

"Three points off the lee bow, sir."

"Raise up your wheel. Steady!"

"Steady, sir."

"Mast-head ahoy! Do you see that whale now?"

"Ay, ay, sir! A school of sperm whales! There she blows! There she breaches!"

"Sing out! Sing out every time!"

"Ay, ay, sir! There she blows! There—there—*thar'* she blows—bowes—bo-o-o-s!"

"How far off!"

"Two miles and a half!"

"Thunder and lightning! so near! Call all hands!"

Boats Away!

"Clew up the fore-t'gallant-sail—there! belay! Hard down your wheel! Haul aback the main yard! Get your tubs in your boats. Bear a hand! Clear your falls! Stand by all to lower! All ready?"

"All ready, sir!"

"Lower away!"

Down went the boats with a splash. Each boat's crew sprang over the rail, and in an instant the larboard, starboard, and waist boats were manned. There was great rivalry in getting the start. The waist-boat got off in pretty good time; and away went all three, dashing the water high over their bows.

. . .

"Line your oars, boys, and pull ahead—(a lapse of two or three minutes)—pull ahead, I tell you, why don't ye—Oh, how they lay, heads and points, look at 'em—pull ahead, I tell ye—long and strong, head boat, I say—(an interval of about 60 seconds)—every man do his best—lay back, I tell ye (fiercely)—why don't ye spring—don't let that boat pass ye (despondingly)—spring, I tell ye (authoritatively) there, there they be, round and round with 'em, for God's sake, pull ahead (entreatingly)—(lapse of a few seconds)—everything—everything I've got in my chest I'll give ye, do spring boys, let's go on first. Now then, back to the thwarts, give her the touch; I feel ye (encouragingly)—five seas off, but five seas off, spring!—3-oar side best; pull all, pull every son of you (boisterously)—I'll give you all my tobacco, everything I've got— look at her, O, what a hump, and slow as night—don't you look round (passionately)—I tell you she don't blow, she only whiffs it out—at the end of your thwarts, pull, and we'll be on this rising— she's an 80-barrel whale; there she mills; by jingo she's heading to leeward; a large fellow separate from the school (shoal)—why the harry don't you pull—now do boys, do your best, won't you (soothingly)—I tell you we are jam on to her! One minute more!"

Harpooner

"Half a minute!—O, boys, if you want to see your sweethearts, if you want to see Nantucket (with emotion), pull ahead—spring, b—t ye, that whale will shorten our voyage six months—I tell you we gain her fast—now's the time—mills still-heading to leeward—slap on to her in a moment—harpooner stand by—all my tobacco—all my clothes—everything that I possess—pull— O, what a whale (softly)—I've hove my soul out—harpooner— harpooner—harpooner . . . —one minute more, lay back; spring half a minute more; all my tobacco, a double share of grog—we are in her wake—(whispers) make no noise with your oars—STAND UP HARPOONER—pull the rest—GIVE IT HER SOLID!

. . . Stern, stern I tell ye (loudly)—stern all, stern like the devil—stern, and get clear of the whale—"

Nantucket Sleigh Ride

. . . The same moment something went hot and hissing along every one of their wrists. It was the magical line. An instant before, Stubb had swiftly caught two additional turns with it round the loggerhead, whence, by reason of its increased rapid circlings, a hempen blue smoke now jetted up and mingled with the steady fumes from his pipe.

"Wet the line! wet the line!" cried Stubb to the tub oarsman (him seated by the tub) who, snatching off his hat, dashed the seawater into it. More turns were taken, so that the line began holding its place. The boat now flew through the boiling water like a shark all fins. Stubb and Tashtego here changed places—stem for stern—a staggering business truly in that rocking commotion.

From the vibrating line extending the entire length of the upper part of the boat, and from its now being more tight than a harp-string, you would have thought the craft had two keels—one cleaving the water, the other the air—as the boat churned on through both opposing elements at once.

A continual cascade played at the bows; a ceaseless whirling eddy in her wake; and, at the slightest motion from within, even but of a little finger, the vibrating, cracking craft canted over her spasmodic gunwale into the sea. Thus they rushed; each man with might and main clinging to his seat, to prevent being tossed to the foam; and the tall form of Tashtego at the steering oar crouching almost double, in order to bring down his centre of gravity. Whole Atlantics and Pacifics seemed passed as they shot on their way, till at length the whale somewhat slackened his flight.

"Haul in—haul in!" cried Stubb to the bowsman, and, facing round towards the whale, all hands began pulling the boat up to him, while yet the boat was being towed on.

Fighting Whale

Then all in one welded commotion came an invisible push from astern, while forward the boat seemed striking on a ledge; a gush of scalding vapor shot up near by; something rolled and tumbled like an earthquake beneath us. The whole crew were half suffocated as they were tossed helter-skelter into the white curdling cream of the squall. Squall, whale, and harpoon had all blended together; and the whale, merely grazed by the iron, escaped. Swimming round the boat we picked up the floating oars, and lashing them across the gunwale, tumbled back to our places. There we sat up to our knees in the sea, the water covering every rib and plank, so that to our downward gazing eyes the suspended craft seemed a coral boat grown up to us from the bottom of the ocean.

The wind increased to a howl; the waves dashed their bucklers together; the whole squall roared, forked, and cracked around us. . . .

"Curses, He's Gone"

Suddenly the waters around them slowly swelled in broad circles; then quickly upheaved, as if sideways sliding from a submerged berg of ice, rising swiftly to the surface. A low rumbling sound was heard, a subterraneous hum; and then all held their breaths; as bedraggled with trailing ropes, and harpoons, and lances, a vast form shot lengthwise, but obliquely from the sea. Shrouded in a thin drooping veil of mist, it hovered for a moment in the rainbowed air; and then fell swamping back into the deep. Crushed thirty feet upwards, the waters flashed for an instant like heaps of fountains, then brokenly sank in a shower of flakes, leaving the circling surface creamed like new milk round the marble trunk of the whale.

. . .

The attentive ship having descried the whole fight, again came bearing down to the rescue, and dropping a boat, picked up the floating mariners, tubs, oars, and whatever else could be caught at, and safely landed them on her decks. Some sprained shoulders, wrists, and ankles; livid contusions; wrenched harpoons and lances; inextricable intricacies of rope! shattered oars and planks; all these were there; but no fatal or even serious ill seemed to have befallen any one.

The Song of a Ship

Ships are the nearest things to dreams that hands have ever made,
For somewhere deep in their oaken hearts the soul of a song is laid;
A soul that sings with the ship along through plunging hills of blue,
And fills her canvas cups of white with winds that drive her through.
For how could a nail and a piece of wood, tied with a canvas thread,
Become a nymph on moon-washed paths if the soul of the ship
   were fled?

Her bosom throbs as her lover's arms clasp her in fond embrace,
And the joyous kiss of briny lips is fresh on her maiden face.
No storm can smother the hempen song that wells in her laughing throat—
Small wonder then that men go mad for the love of the sea and a boat.
For the singing sheet is a siren sweet that tugs at the hearts of men,
And down to the sea they must go once more though they
   never come back again.

MAP OF THE

CITY of CANTON
& ADJACENT ISLANDS.

Statute Miles

"Land Ho!"–China

. . . And finally there was the call from the lookout, "Land ho!" That off the bow was not another island, but the mainland, China. The ship came in through crowds of noisy, slatternly coastal sampans and big, clumsy-hulled junks. Typa Island was on the port hand, behind it Macao where the ship might later touch for cargo. Grand Lema Island in the Ladrones group was dead ahead and the captain brought the ship up into the wind to take the pilot aboard.

The pilot during most of the clipper years was a little, brown and extremely polite man. He grinned as he boarded from his sampan that his mate handled smartly enough and which had two wide-gazing eyes painted on the bows. His orders to the ship's wheelsman were exact and clear, and the captain stood and listened without objection and the wheelsman sent the smooth spokes over glistening and the ship had found her wind, swung up into Canton Bay.

The bay was broad, and long, and once the ship was squared away on the new tack past the Ladrones shoals the men could stand by the rail and gawk for a bit and listen to the old-time bosun. The big island over to starboard was Lantao; past that was Hong Kong. Up here on the starboard bow was Tonkoo roadstead, and the skinny little island fine on the starboard bow was called Lintin and in Chinese it meant "Solitary Nail."

Opium

The bosun hitched at his pants and pointed at the vessels in under the lee of Lintin; he was ready to impress his listeners.

He described the three hulks as British-owned. They received the opium carried from India, and from here the stuff was taken in local craft up the rivers and bays and along the coast, far into North China. It was all against Chinese law, so there was a lot of graft among the officials supposed to stop the trade.

The clipper sailors stood still, remembering old, fantastic fo'c'sle stories. They half-doubted the bosun; he seemed too certain. But there was little doubt about the hulks. It was obvious that not long ago they had been sturdy ships which had been roofed over in dockyard style. Tile chimneys rose through the roofs, and there were verandas where flowers bloomed in rows of pots. Along the hull, though, the gun ports were triced up, and the muzzles of the heavy-caliber pieces showed. Lookouts kept a watch on deck, and they wore side arms.

British captains were aboard the receiving hulks, the bosun said, and they were tough nuts who knew how to keep hold of the fortunes they had aboard and hold their crews in line. The crews were made up of Lascars, but the carpenters and the boatmen attached to each hulk were Chinese. The big, two-masted Chinese boats made fast alongside the hulks were called in the local style centipedes and scrambling dragons, and when they were under weigh fifty men rowed them. It was the centipedes and scrambling dragons that distributed the stuff for the native smugglers up in the back creeks and coves. The smugglers paid cash, sycee silver, to the receiving hulk captains for what they bought. Then, the smugglers collected in return from the back-country agents.

The clipper crew felt a kind of awe. This was crime on a scale beyond their immediate comprehension. Opium to them, who welcomed anything named whiskey, was a dread drug. It bore a reputation of evil power beyond man's will to conquer, and those who used the stuff soon became weaklings and fools, and worse. But the neat, alertly guarded receiving hulks, the big Chinese river craft with their fifty oarsmen apiece and the fleet of clippers at anchor the other side of the island gave an impression of deliberate military organization. The scene had no resemblance to a smuggler base anywhere else in the world.

The opium clippers lay to with plenty of cable in under Lintin. They were barks of about three hundred tons, with an extremely rakish rig, black-hulled with a white gun strake that carried ten ports to a side. The cannons were run back in the gear, but they gleamed from polishing, and the mate on watch came down the deck with a strut, let go a shout for his bosun that made some of the sailors aboard the inward-bound clipper jump.

The American clipper bosun described that ship and her mate as British. But a number of vessels in the opium fleet were American-owned, he said, and had American officers aboard. The crews were Lascars and Portuguese seacunnies from Macao, who got good pay and should, because of the risks. A man was never really off watch in an opium smuggler, slept with one eye open and his ears stretched tight.

Up the Pearl River

Now the inward-bounder was once more in narrow waters as she reached the head of the bay and the Pearl River mouth. There was no more time for talk. The men were sent fast from the braces to the sheets as the pilot maneuvered her up through the Bogue. This was the defile which for centuries had been held inviolable by the Chinese because of the forts they had built on each side of it. But in the war brought against them in 1840 by the British the forts had been found weak, almost useless. Their massive cannons were in fixed positions inside the embrasures, and as the British squadron passed upstream the ships in line whipped enfilading fire that created terrific casualties. Mandarins who commanded the forts caught up their dragon-decorated robes and ran, left the forts locked with the coolie troops inside to be found by the British landing parties. It was a war fought over the right of an alien people, the British, to introduce opium into China, and it was called the Opium War, and from the beginning the Chinese with their lack of knowledge of Western methods of warfare never had a chance.

Hauling, making fast, then hauling again, the clipper crew stared over the bulwarks at the empty, battered forts and wondered about their history. But all that the new men could tell themselves was they had never before seen a country like this, no matter where the ships had taken them. The clipper was past Tiger Island and out of the Bogue. Here before them was the wide Canton plain.

It contained a beauty which was much different from that of the sea; still it held the men. They gazed at it in rapt delight while the mate and the bosun shouted. The spaces were immense, and the light so brilliant that the entire landscape seemed to shimmer. Rice paddies a delicate, soft green in color stretched across the plain until it was closed in upon by a bowl of very pale but sharp, blue hills. There were villages, huddled and cramped and brown-toned, in between the paddies, and once in a while a big country house with peaked gateways and corner timbers and russet-tiled roofs. Where the land rose to a slope, there was always a pagoda, layer on layer of fretted and chromatically painted wood, the roofs built so that they lifted in snub-nosed arches to the sun.

But there were almost no trees, and in the sheer brilliance of the light people could be seen miles away. They were so busy they created a kind of constant hum, like large bees, the sailors thought. The Chinese out there on the plain were wading thigh-deep in the paddies. They were scrabbling in the fields with hoes, or whacking the bony hips of water buffalo, fishing in the brooks, rowing along the rivers in hundreds of peculiar craft, herding pigs and chickens and ducks over the roads. Most of them wore wide-brimmed, high-peaked, rattan rain hats and faded blue cotton clothing. Women carried small children on their backs. Men strode stooped with the weight of their carrying poles, buckets or baskets at each end, the tight trousers rucked at the calves where the muscles bulged, and under the hat brims the faces were concave in shadow and sad, yet calm.

Whampoa

The ship was rounding up for one of the river bars and now the wind was against her and she was almost aground. The sailors forgot the landscape and ran to pass heaving lines to the six-oared boats that the pilot had called alongside. Hawsers followed the heaving lines; the coolies in the boats bent to their sweeps and the sweep blades curved with the strain in the brown water. The ship moved, bumped the bar and was over, and the captain told the pilot, "Good fella, Charley!"

"Hiyah," the pilot said, his expression unchanged.

Above the upper bar, standing on an easterly course, the ship passed the Six Flat Islands where storks stood one-legged and incurious, and Dane Island, and Whampoa, and over that the sailors could see the tall, varnished spars of row upon row of ships. This was it, *Wang-po*, as the Chinese said the word; Whampoa to the Westerners, still the Yellow Anchorage. Upriver thirteen miles away was Canton, the City of Rams.

The ship braced her yards once more and was clear of Whampoa Island. Here in a great crescent, all at anchor, the ships lay, sixty, seventy of them, and many the finest clippers in the world. The captain took the ship from the pilot; he had his own, final decision to make when he anchored her. The mate stood at the bow, staring overside, the carpenter and the bosun near him, some of the smart hands right in back of them by the windlass.

The captain looked over the fleet, and caught the glint of long-glass brass as the masters of the other ships studied his seamanship. He had all of the canvas off her except the foresail and a jib; her signal flags were run up and secured; the man at the wheel had her exactly where the captain wanted her. The captain looked to port and starboard, measuring between the two big East Indiamen berthed there. Then, a tremor of nervous fatigue in his knees, but his voice very steady, he told the mate in a quick, strong cry: "Let go your anchor, sir!"

Sampans

The crew was not allowed to go to Hog Lane till the next day. But even before the anchor had taken ground the washee-washee girls were around the ship in their boats. The girls were big and bosomy and smiling. They formed a gay flotilla in their twenty-foot-long boats that were decked with split bamboo and had neat curtains along the sides. They handled the boats with skill and they recognized the mate where he stood on the fo'c'slehead. Their calls were lustily repeated, and the mate laughed as he listened.

"Ah, you missee chiefee mate, how you doa? I saavez you long time, when you catchee Whampoa last time. How missee capitainee? I saavez him werry wen. You saavez my? I make mendee all same your shirtee last time."

This was straight fact, and the mate sent a sailor aft for his gear that needed washing and mending. But then he quietly warned the new members of the crew about attempts to make contact with the washee-washee girls. Their actions were watched, he said, by hundreds of Chinese officials who patrolled the river. The girls would be squeegeed—severely fined and beaten—if found in any sort of intimacy with foreigners. After dark, though, things were different. The bosun picked up what the mate left unsaid and pointed off past the washboats to another, smaller flotilla.

Those over there were egg-boats, the bosun said. The pairs of girls who sculled them were a bit less robust than the laundresses; they wore red ribbons in their double pigtails, and artificial flowers

in their hair. The boats they sculled were only about eight feet long, more raft than anything else, with an egg-shaped bamboo structure amidships to keep a passenger out of the rain. After dark, no squeegee, the bosun told the new crew members. Down the anchor cable was the way, when the ship swung and hauled in slack. The egg-boats would be waiting, and a man did not have to call or shout.

Excitement kept mounting throughout the dusk and on into the night. It was the usual symptom of channel fever shown aboard any ship after a long passage, and the mates and the captain paid little attention to the splashes, the sighs, cries and expostulations of the bow. The captain was busy with the procession of Chinese officials who had been coming over the side ever since the ladder had been lowered. The squeeze had begun, and *cumshaw*—literally, in translation, "golden sand"—was flowing across the cabin table.

The first official up the side was the *compradore*, a man with a very important function. He represented the Co-hong merchants ashore who had given security for the ship to the Emperor, and the *compradore* was responsible for her and her crew during all of her time in the river. The *compradore* was stooped and grizzled by the complexity of his duties, yet he could smile as he fingered his thin mustache, and he responded without complaint to the name of Acow, which wasn't his name at all, but a gross corruption of it. He started his work aboard by ordering a supply of fresh meat and vegetables for the ship, then sat on the cabin settee with the captain and in the extraordinarily clumsy pidgin English which was their only common language talked over the details of the voyage.

Up on deck, the mates held Jack Hoppo in conversation. Jack was Acow's guard and assistant and a good deal more. He was supposed to stop any smuggling that might take place between the ship, a passing boat, or another visiting official bound for shore. But Jack, for a small sprinkling of *cumshaw*, would cross the deck, look for an agreed-upon time over at Dane Island, and only turn his head long after the smuggler was gone. When there were police boats near in the river Jack had his own ideas about the salvage of illicit cargo, and was quite imaginative and adroit, for an added fee.

The mate set the crew to work right at dawn. They rigged the cargo tackle and opened up the hatches for the coolie gangs that would come aboard soon to begin the discharge. From the ship, the cargo would go into lighters and then be towed up to Jackass Point at Canton and put in the warehouses of the Co-hong merchants who transacted the ship's business. But the crew hardly looked at the coolie gangs or the lighters. The bosun had just told them that this was the end of work for the day and they were to knock off and get squared away for Hog Lane.

Liberty

On a typical day for this liberty they washed and shaved and dressed, shouting across the fo'c'sle at each other in a mood almost like frenzy. Then they mustered aft, drew their pay from the captain, put the cutter in the water and swarmed aboard her and took their places on the thwarts. The mate in charge of them and the boat was not too happy. He had seen the consequences of other Hog Lane outings. But he also wanted to visit Canton, and was sick of the ship. When the cutter was cast off from the davit falls and the men had locked their oars, he told them to give for him, hard.

They rowed joyously at first, looking up with renewed interest at the great, clumsy, double-decker East Indiamen with their checkerboard black and white sides whose gun ports and design and sail plan had not changed since Trafalgar. Some of the men made loud comments about Limejuicers and the kind of washtubs they sailed. But they received no answers from on deck and the current was rapid and there was plenty, really too much, to be seen along the river.

Huge, teak-hulled, coasting junks that the mate said were in from Java and Manila and Sumatra and Borneo and Singapore and Hong Kong came up breasting the current and went to the anchor and swung, banged from position the smaller salt junks in from the southwest coast. There were passenger junks bound down for sea, all gilt scrolls and yawning dragons, big, popped eyes on the bows, firecrackers going off, men whom the mate identified as priests waving joss sticks and throwing little strips of varicolored paper over the side. There were chopboats which went past with a lick of white water at the oar blades pulled by seventy men. Those, the mate said, were on government business. The boat that carried men on deck armed with swords belonged to a mandarin. She was called a war dragon.

The men could only nod. They were dazed. It was as if the river had become for them an immense cornucopia from which poured color, light, sound, sensation too potent for them to register. The silk pennants streaming from the mandarin boat, the double-decked oars that flashed in perfect cadence, even the more or less familiar bulk of the East Indiamen were already a confusion in the mind.

Here across the tawny swiftness of the river was an entire city of boats. Shop boats, and store boats, and those that sold flowers and toys and trousers. Barbers had their own craft and twanged their tweezers to announce their trade. Boats with singing birds aboard, and boats like farms with chickens on deck and ducks in the water alongside. Small, fast ferries called tankas, and big ones with jabbering, waving, craning passengers, and houseboats gilded and painted, scrolled, and boats that carried dung and were called Night Flower Boats.

The men shook their heads and blinked. Almost as though in a state of shock, they stopped rowing. The cutter drifted. But the mate at the tiller understood. He had seen this before. It was time for a breather and a bit of grog, he said, the grog with the compliments of the captain.

They thanked him and shoved their hats back and drank slowly, their tobacco wads held in the palms of their hands. But the bosun was gazing in at the northern bank. The boats there were different, even smelled different. The new men recognized them without being told; those were the Flower Boats, the floating brothels whose women served the river and shore population of Canton.

Now the women were staring down at the cutter as the sailors began to row again and passed close alongside. They leaned forth, dazzling, startling figures in their silks and brocades and heavy

jewelry, and smiled, tittered, gracefully gestured in an invitation that no egg-boat girl could give. These boats were alive with chromatic paint; the banisters and rails were gilded; the ropes along deck were of silk; flower pots lined the roofs; the window shades of the women's apartments were decorated in bird designs, and live birds kept in cages under the eaves sweetly sang.

If a foreigner boarded one of the Flower Boats, the mate said solemnly, he ended up in the river. Foreigners had tried it, and their bodies had been found, bound hand and foot. So, hang on for Hog Lane.

Hog Lane

But there was still another hour to go, and soon after that, still below Dutch Folly Fort, the men were forced to bring their oars aboard and use paddles. All the way to the water steps at Jackass Point, the mate said, the river was too thick in traffic for anything else to be used. The police kept lanes open between the huge junks aboard which in tenement fashion thousands of people lived.

Sampans, egg-boats, tankas, lorchas were tied up at every intersection, and the cutter crew pushed past with boat hooks, were cursed for scratching paintwork. Men and women and big and little children looked out from the doors and windows. Curses were called louder; garbage was flung, and bilge water, and dung. Children prompted by their elders stood on deck and went through graphic gestures. They seized themselves by the tops of their heads, pulled their heads upward, then made sawing motions across their throats. The bosun called them Celestial sons-of-bitches in pidgin, but it only increased the ferocity of the pantomime.

The men grunted, paddling hard to enter a strip of open water. The famous and square-built city was right beyond, past the upward thrust of Honan Island. The city's walls were tall, the gates broad and high, the men saw as they stared, and the mate said that within the city a million people lived and that each wall was a mile long. Here dead ahead was the port where the sampans and junks tied up, and now the cutter crew could see the tall flagstaffs at the foreign factories. Those were over at the western end of the port, across a small stretch of ground, British, American, Dutch and French.

When the cutter was secured to the big iron rings at the water steps the men were so eager they almost ran. The mate let them go in charge of the bosun. They scampered like burly, outsize children through the prim shrubbery in front of the British factory and knocked down dozing Chinese loungers on Respondentia Walk and then, with the bosun leading, disappeared into Hog Lane. The mate kept on toward the American factory on the other side of the walk. He could imagine the yells of welcome being given by Ben Bobstay, Old Jemmy Apoo, Tom Bowline, Jolly Jack, Young Tom and Old Sam's Brother and the other outstanding grogshop owners on Hog Lane.

The owners had discovered that they were invariably successful when they greeted the newcomers with, "Fine day, Jack! How you do, old boy?"

168

Mouths Were Made for Tankards

Oh some are fond of dancing, and some are fond of dice,
And some are all for red lips, and pretty lasses' eyes;
But a right Jamaica puncheon is a finer prize
    To the old bold mate of Henry Morgan.

Oh some that's good and godly ones they hold that it's a sin
To troll the jolly bowl around, and let the dollars spin;
But I'm for toleration and for drinking at an inn,
    Says the old bold mate of Henry Morgan.

Oh some are sad and wretched folk that go in silken suits,
And there's a mort of wicked rogues that live in good reputes;
So I'm for drinking honestly, and dying in my boots,
    Like an old bold mate of Henry Morgan.

Oh some are fond of red wine, and some are fond of white,
And some are all for dancing by the pale moonlight;
But rum alone's the tipple, and the heart's delight
    Of the old bold mate of Henry Morgan.

Oh some are fond of Spanish wine, and some are fond of French,
And some'll swallow tay and stuff fit only for a wench;
But I'm for right Jamaica till I roll beneath the bench,
    Says the old bold mate of Henry Morgan.

Oh some are fond of fiddles, and a song well sung,
And some are all for music for to lilt upon the tongue;
But mouths were made for tankards, and for sucking at the bung,
    Says the old bold mate of Henry Morgan.

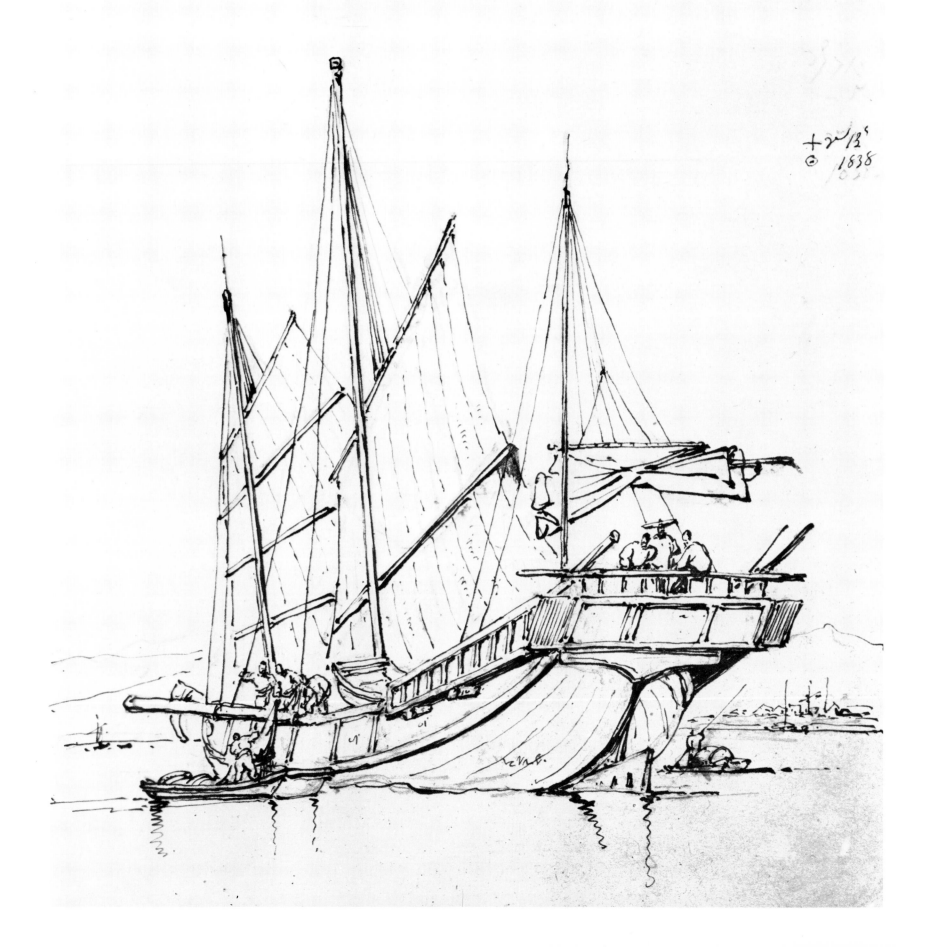

The Chinese Junk

Once a pair of savages found a stranded tree.
      (One-piecee stick-pidgin—two-piecee man.
Straddle-um—paddle-um—push-um off to sea.
      That way Foleign Debbil-boat began.)
But before, and before, and ever so long before
      Any shape of sailing-craft was known,
The Junk and Dhow had a stern and a bow,
      And a mast and a sail of their own—ahoy! alone!
      As they crashed across the Oceans on their own!

Once there was a pirate-ship, being blown ashore—
      (Plitty soon pilum up, s'posee no can tack.
Seven-piecee stlong man pullum sta'boa'd oar.
      That way bling her head alound and sail-o back.)
But before, and before, and ever so long before
      Grand Commander Noah took the wheel,
The Junk and the Dhow, though they look like anyhow,
      Had rudders reaching deep below their keel—ahoy! akeel!
      As they laid the Eastern Seas beneath their keel!

Once there was a galliot yawing in a tide.
      (Too much foolee side-slip. How can stop?
Man catchee tea-box lid—lasha longaside.
      That way make her plenty glip and sail first-chop.)
But before, and before, and ever so long before
      Any such contrivances were used,
The whole Confucian sea-board had standardised the lee-board.
      And hauled it up or dropped it as they choosed—
          or chose—or chused!
      According to the weather, when they cruised!

Once there was a caravel in a beam-sea roll—
      (Ca'go shiftee—alla dliftee—no can livee long.
S'posum' nail-o boa'd acloss—makee ploper hol'?
      That way, ca'go sittum still, an' ship mo' stlong.)
But before, and before, and ever so long before
      Any square-rigged vessel hove in sight,
The Canton deep-sea craft carried bulkheads fore and aft,
      And took good care to keep 'em water-tight—atite—atite!
      From Amboyna to the Great Australian Bight!

Once there was a sailor-man singing just this way—
      (Too muchee yowl-o, sickum best flend!
Singee all-same pullee lope—haul and belay!
      Hully up and coilum down an'—bite off end!)
But before, and before, and ever so long before
      Any sort of chanty crossed our lips,
The Junk and the Dhow, though they look like anyhow,
      Were the Mother and the Father of all Ships—
          ahoy!—a'ships!
      And of half the new inventions in our Ships!
      From Tarifa to Formosa in our Ships!
          From Socotra to Selankhor of the windlass and the anchor,
      And the Navigators' Compass in our Ships—ahoy!
          —our Ships!
(O, hully up and coilum down and —bite—off—end!)

GEORGE CHINNERY / RUDYARD KIPLING 171

172   MONTAGUE DAWSON / C. FOX SMITH

By the Old Pagoda Anchorage

By the old Pagoda Anchorage they lay full fifteen strong,
And their spars were like a forest, and their names
    were like a song,
Fiery Cross *and* Falcon *there*
Lay with Spindrift, *doomed and fair,*
And Sir Lancelot of a hundred famous fights with wind and wave:
Belted Will *and* Hallowe'en
With Leander *there were seen,*
And Ariel *and* Titania *and* Robin Hood *the brave:*
Thyatira *of the lovely name and proud* Thermopylae.

By the old Pagoda Anchorage when clippers sailed the sea,
Racing home to London River—
Carry on for London River—
Crack her on for London River with her chests of China tea!

By the old Pagoda Anchorage (it's many a year ago!)
A sight it was to see them with their decks like drifted snow,
And their brasses winking bright,
And the gleaming gold and white
Of the carven kings and maidens on each slim and soaring bow,
And the high and slender spars
Humming shanties to the stars,
And the hulls whose speed and staunchness
    are a dead man's secret now—

The ships so brave and beautiful that never more shall be,
By the old Pagoda Anchorage when clippers sailed the sea,
Racing home to London River—
Crack her on for London River—
Carry on for London River with her chests of China tea!

By the old Pagoda Anchorage the clippers lie no more,
There is silence on the river, there is quiet on the shore,
And the silted channels seem
Still to murmur as in dream
Of the tea ships in their glory, lifting seaward on the tide,
All the strong and fair and fleet,
By those shores that used to meet,
And the valiant master mariners that walked
    their decks in pride,

By the old Pagoda Anchorage when clippers sailed the sea,
Logging fourteen on a bowline, ay, and
    seventeen running free,
Racing home for London River—
Crack her on for London River—
Carry on for London River with her chests of China tea!

"All Hands Up Anchor!"

"All hands up anchor!" When that order was given, how we sprang to the bars, and heaved round that capstan; every man a Goliath, every tendon a hawser!—round, round it spun like a sphere, keeping time with our feet to the time of the fife till the cable was straight up and down, and the ship with her nose in the water.

"Heave and pall! Unship your bars, and make sail!" It was done: barmen, nippermen, tierres, veerers, idlers and all, scrambled up the ladder to the braces and halyards; while like monkeys in palm trees, the sail-loosers ran out on those broad boughs, our yards; and down fell the sails like white clouds from the ether—topsails, top-gallants, and royals; and away we ran with the halyards, till every sheet was distended.

"Once more to the bars! Heave, my hearties, heave hard!" With a jerk and a yerk, we broke ground; and up to our bows came several thousand pounds of old iron, in the shape of our ponderous anchor.

Tacking Out

The weather-leech of the topsail shivers,
    The bowlines strain, and the lee-shrouds slacken,
The braces are taut, the lithe boom quivers,
    And the waves with the coming squall-cloud blacken.

Open one point on the weather-bow,
    Is the lighthouse tall on Fire Island Head.
There's a shade of doubt on the captain's brow,
    And the pilot watches the heaving lead.

I stand at the wheel, and with eager eye
    To sea and to sky and to shore I gaze,
Till the muttered order of "Full and by!"
    Is suddenly changed for "Full for stays!"

The ship bends lower before the breeze,
    As her broadside fair to the blast she lays;
And she swifter springs to the rising seas,
    As the pilot calls, "Stand by for stays!"

It is silence all, as each in his place,
    With the gathered coil in his hardened hands,
By tack and bowline, by sheet and brace,
    Waiting the watchword impatient stands.

And the light on Fire Island Head draws near,
    As, trumpet-winged, the pilot's shout
From his post on the bowsprit's heel I hear,
    With the welcome call of "Ready! About!"

No time to spare! It is touch and go;
    And the captain growls, "Down helm! hard down!"
As my weight on the whirling spokes I throw,
    While heaven grows black with the storm-cloud's frown.

High o'er the knight-heads flies the spray,
    As we meet the shock of the plunging sea;
And my shoulder stiff to the wheel I lay,
    As I answer, "Ay, ay, sir! Ha-a-rd a-lee!"

With the swerving leap of a startled steed
    The ship flies fast in the eye of the wind,
The dangerous shoals on the lee recede,
    And the headland white we have left behind.

The topsails flutter, the jibs collapse,
    And belly and tug at the groaning cleats;
The spanker slats, and the mainsail flaps;
    And thunders the order, "Tacks and sheets!"

Mid the rattle of blocks and the tramp of the crew,
    Hisses the rain of the rushing squall:
The sails are aback from clew to clew,
    And now is the moment for "Mainsail, haul!"

And the heavy yards, like a baby's toy,
    By fifty strong arms are swiftly swung:
She holds her way, and I look with joy
    For the first white spray o'er the bulwarks flung.

"Let go, and haul!" 'Tis the last command,
    And the head-sails fill to the blast once more:
Astern and to leeward lies the land,
    With its breakers white on the shingly shore.

What matters the reef, or the rain, or the squall?
    I steady the helm for the open sea;
The first mate clamors, "Belay, there, all!"
    And the captain's breath once more comes free.

And so off shore let the good ship fly;
    Little care I how the gusts may blow,
In my fo'castle bunk, in a jacket dry.
    Eight bells have struck, and my watch is below.

Malayan Pirates

Just before daylight Captain Archer came to me, and roused me, saying that there were some suspicious looking sails in sight. I sprang up and could readily see with my night glass two proas coming out from under the land a few miles to the northward. I at once ordered all hands called, and as the wind had got round northeast, although still light, I immediately got under weigh and made all sail. Meanwhile the proas were standing down toward us, and as the daylight broke it was evident that they were full of men.

The *Mystic*, as was quite common in those days, carried a couple of 24 pounders, with a fair amount of ammunition, and we had, in addition to the ship's muskets, the rifles I had purchased at Valparaiso. So we were unusually well prepared in that direction, and, having Captain Archer's crew, we were nearly doubly manned. Still, so far as force was concerned, we were outnumbered by the Malays in the proas five to one. It would never do to let them get on board of us, for in a hand-to-hand fight we should have much the worst of it.

Captain Archer and I agreed to keep the proas at bay with the 24 pounders. Captain Archer went aft to take over the wheel and luff the ship, as I prepared the guns.

"Put your helm down, my man; look out, Captain Kelson! Let draw the headsheets! Meet her with the helm; meet her!" The *Mystic* came up in the wind, the head sails flapped; I watched my chance, got a good sight with the gun, which was loaded with a solid shot, and pulled the lock-string! As the smoke blew to leeward I sprang on the rail, and as the ship payed off and the sails filled, the foremast of the leading proas snapped off a few feet above the deck and fell overboard with a great crash dragging with it the heavy lateen sail!

"Good shot, Kelson!" shouted Captain Archer from the poop as our men cheered. We expected the second proa to heave to and go to the assistance of her companion, but she passed her without pausing, and with her sweeps out and heavily manned she bore rapidly down upon us. I ordered the starboard gun run over to the port side and tried several shots at the approaching proa, but, although I hit her once I did not seem to inflict very serious damage. So I then had both 24 pounders loaded with shrapnel and langridge, and determined to fight it out at closer quarters.

Stationing both my officers and the carpenter, who was a splendid shot, on the quarter-deck with rifles, I ordered them to pick off

the men who seemed to be the leaders, and then waited for the approach of the proa.

When the proa had crept up within easy rifle range, I luffed the ship up, as before, and getting a deliberate aim at the crowded deck, depressed the guns and fired them at the word, both at once, point blank, reloading and repeating the dose before the smoke of the first discharge had cleared away. The effect of this murderous fire, at such close quarters, upon the crowd massed upon the proa's deck was terrific, and the slaughter was frightful. Yet by some strange chance, the captain, a tall, vicious-looking Malay, stripped to the waist and waving a naked kreese to encourage his followers, had escaped uninjured, and was shouting to his men, to rally them, with the evident intent of boarding us.

Captain Archer had meanwhile filled our ship away, but the wind was light, and before we had fairly gained headway the proa, with the sweeps out, shot under our starboard quarter, and a grapnel thrown from her caught in our mizzen chains.

The pirate captain at once sprang forward, and, with his kreese in his mouth, scrambled up our side, followed by a score of his men, and gained the poop deck of the ship! Abandoning our battery, we gathered in the waist, and I called to the carpenter to pick off the Malay captain. He nodded, and, taking a careful sight with his rifle, he fired, and the Malayan fell dead among his men. Our other riflemen were meanwhile dropping those of the proa who had followed their captain.

Just then the wind freshened, and by great good fortune the proa's grapnel disengaged itself and she dropped astern. Calling upon my men, we made a dash upon the few remaining Malays and fairly drove them overboard. I then put the helm down, and as we came round on the other tack and gathered headway, I stood down on the proa, a good wrap full, and striking her fair and square amidships cut her to the water's edge.

Our victory was now complete, and as the first proa, having disentangled herself from the wreck of the foremast, was coming down, with sweeps out, to rescue the survivors of her consort, I made all sail and kept on my course, leaving them to their own devices. The 15th of November we passed through the Straits of Sunda and laid our course to the westward.

"A Sailor-Man"

The business of a thorough-bred sailor is a special calling, as much of a regular trade as a carpenter's or lock-smith's. Indeed, it requires considerably more adroitness, and far more versatility of talent.

A thorough sailor must understand much of other avocations. He must be a bit of an embroiderer, to work fanciful collars of hempen lace about the shrouds; he must be something of a weaver, to weave mats of rope-yarns for lashings to the boats; he must have a touch of millinery, so as to tie graceful bows and knots, such as *Matthew Walker's roses*, and *Turk's heads*; he must be a bit of a musician, in order to sing out at the halyards; he must be a sort of jeweler, to set dead-eyes in the standing rigging; he must be a carpenter, to enable him to make a jury-mast out of a yard in case of emergency; he must be a sempstress, to darn and mend the sails; a ropemaker, to twist *marline* and *Spanish foxes;* a blacksmith, to make hooks and thimbles for the blocks: in short, he must be a sort of Jack of all trades, in order to master his own. And this, perhaps, in a greater or less degree, is pretty much the case with all things else; for you know nothing till you know all; which is the reason we never know any thing.

A sailor, also, in working at the rigging, uses special tools peculiar to his calling—*fids*, *serving-mallets*, *toggles*, *prickers*, *marlingspikes*, *palms*, *heavers*, and many more. The smaller sort he generally carries with him from ship to ship in a sort of canvas reticule.

The estimation in which a ship's crew hold the knowledge of such accomplishments as these, is expressed in the phrase they apply to one who is a clever practitioner. To distinguish such a mariner from those who merely *'hand, reef, and steer,'* that is, run aloft, furl sails, haul ropes, and stand at the wheel, they say he is *'a sailor-man';* which means that he not only knows how to reef a topsail, but is an artist in the rigging.

WILLIAM LEE-HANKEY / JOHN MASEFIELD

Memories

All the sheets are clacking, all the blocks are whining,
The sails are frozen stiff and the wetted decks are shining;
The reef's in the topsails, and it's coming on to blow,
And I think of the dear girl I left long ago.

Grey were her eyes, and her hair was long and bonny,
Golden was her hair, like the wild bees' honey.
And I was but a dog, and a mad one to despise,
The gold of her hair and the grey of her eyes.

There's the sea before me, and my home's behind me,
And beyond there the strange lands where nobody will mind me,
No one but the girls with the paint upon their cheeks,
Who sell away their beauty to whomsoever seeks.

There'll be drink and women there, and songs and laughter,
Peace from what is past and from all that follows after;
And a fellow will forget how a woman lies awake,
Lonely in the night watch crying for his sake.

Black it blows and bad and it howls like slaughter,
And the ship she shudders as she takes the water.
Hissing flies the spindrift like a windblown smoke,
And I think of a woman and a heart I broke.

The Struggle at the Wheel–1

I grappled with the kicking fury of the spokes. In a minute I was in a lather of sweat, though ice was already forming on my oilskins. A series of shocks ran up my arms, through my shoulders to my jolted spine. I was lifted bodily from my feet, suspended by my stretched hands alone, until a weather-roll of the overborne hull enabled me to catch my booted heel in the stanchion of the wheel-grating, thus securing a purchase which enabled me to master that immediate flurry. Then the ship appeared to recognize my familiar touch; she calmed down, leaned over until I saw the foam-crest piled three feet high above her lee-rail, and snorted straight through the smother like a racehorse.

"Keep her that way!" Captain Fegan approved.

But being at the *Dovenby*'s wheel that night was not a picnic—far from it. Never before under my hands had the ship been so restive. She played possum, affected to be controlled, until she fancied I was lulled into my old belief in her subservience, then—with a crash and a roar she was fighting savagely for her freedom, and not caring how she fought. The tiny glimmer of light in the binnacle showed her restless head swinging four, even five,

points on either side of her allotted course. Once she all but ran away altogether, threatening to broach-to and fall over on her beam ends. Tired out, Skilly aided valiantly, but his shrimp-like weight hardly helped to tip the balance.

"Steering all right?" asked Fegan, coming aft, an unseen presence, from his keen vigil by the poop-rail.

"Ay, ay, sir—a bit frisky!" I boasted.

"Watch her, boy. They're in trouble for'ard there!" He passed to leeward of the binnacle and stood, back to the wheel, grasping the spokes there in an underhand way. "Nip for'ard, you," he instructed Skilly. "Ask the mate how it goes." But Skilly had to wait before essaying that passage. The ship suddenly took the bit in her teeth and rioted ecstatically, as if stung by a Gargantuan horse-fly. She broke away from my hold, she spun Fegan round until his big body was on top of me, crushing me into the deck—or so it seemed—and, swinging her quarter toward the run of the high seas, she pooped. It seemed as if the end had come. Sheer tonnage of icy water crushed me down to my knees. I was turned round, the spokes torn from my hold; a kick of the wheel caused one spoke to hit me excruciatingly under the chin—it was almost a knock-out. Stars spun in my brain. For some reason the heel of the skipper's sea-boot was grinding into my mouth; I felt a tooth snap and then another. It didn't seem to matter a lot; obviously, my dazed senses informed me, she was already sinking; nothing could fetch her up again. Her reserve of buoyancy had been battered out of her.

There was a curiosity as to what death might be like, that was all. One's senses were stunned, so that fear and normal emotions were paralyzed. It was like hovering on the edge of sleep before plunging into blissful unconsciousness.

COMMAND · A.BRISCOE/37

The Struggle at the Wheel – II

But interest in life returned as the stern soared high, hurling Fegan for'ard against the binnacle, round which his limp body seemed to curl. I got upright and grabbed the whirling spokes; savagely I ground them down, ready to snap them like carrots if they refused to come. There is a resistless quality in the human body at such times that is superior to will and muscle. I was blazing angry—crazily so, ready to run berserk.

As Fegan pulled himself upright—he had been hurt inside—lo and behold! Skilly was there, warping himself aft by the rail of the cabin skylight. Whilst we had grappled with the frantic helm he had been washed for'ard, down the ladder, half-way along the main-deck. He said he had been carried clean overboard and washed back again. The ship demanded close watching every minute. Back at the lee-helm Skilly worked like a horse: taking the load from me as I hove up the spokes, standing by for an extra heave as I ran them down. This was no nice steering, with the turn of a spoke either way sufficing to control the blusterous fabric; it meant hard-up and hard-down every time the lubber's point swung past the compass-point which was our designed course.

The *Dovenby* swung until the main yard-arms threatened to dip under the wave-tops on either side. If this swing were countered by savage helm-work, she pitched frantically, dipping her bow under until solid water was surging over the fo'c'sle, or the poop-rail was submerged. Time after time water rose to my armpits, tearing urgently at me; and the rope-lashing I had managed to bowline round my body seemed determined to cut me in halves.

Dawn took me unawares, and, in that latitude, at that time of year, it was a late dawn. It was also ominous in the extreme. There was not a patch of brightness anywhere—simply a lurid, low-hanging canopy of ragged cloud over all—the tattered edges joining the up-leaping seas to close in a very narrow horizon.

Sometimes the screaming squalls beat the rugged wave-tops flat, tearing them into slashing spindrift which laced the deep troughs into a patterned milkiness. The ship handled better in these squalls, giving me and Skilly a breathing-space which was sorely needed. But just as one became aware of momentary surcease the full fury of the squall died, the waves piled mountainously, and the ship was at her old cavorting tricks again, seeming intent on tying a Carrick bend in herself.

It was a long time before details along the decks and aloft grew out of the filthy yellow-greyness that was daylight. Water crashed aboard pitilessly over the fore brace-blocks, the main and the mizen alike. Up aloft all was dishevelment. Much sail had been shortened after darkness fell, and it had been clumsily stowed, because of the high wind-force and the cold, which had frozen the drenched canvas into the likeness of armor-plating. There were "Irish pennants" blowing loose in bights to leeward all over. What the crew were doing I could not see.

No smoke came from the galley—the funnel had gone overboard long before. The lee lifeboat had vanished, too—the davits swinging drunkenly. The dinghy, normally stowed on the forehouse, was simply a faggot of broken staves—a sea had fallen and broken it small. Some of the washports had been torn from their hinges. Half the ropes, braces and downhauls and sheets, had been washed through the scupper-holes, and trailed overside like fantastic weeds. The ship was disheveled and forlorn. Something was missing from her bulwarks, too—abreast the fore-hatch the cargo-doors had been torn away, and ropes had been laced across the gap to safeguard the crew.

Just then Skilly collapsed, utterly worn-out. I'd noticed a slackening in the aid he gave me, but had been too busy to give him much attention.

"'Nother hand to the lee-wheel!" bellowed Fegan, hurrying to the poop-break, whence he returned to lift the cadet like an infant and carry him—not to the cabin—but to the saturated half-deck. No favors were shown to human weakness aboard the *Dovenby!*

He who came was an able seaman, one of the best men aboard, the first to scramble aloft at the call, the last to descend; quick to lay out on a scrabbling yard-arm, a leading shantyman, apt to drink to excess in port, and to work like four men at sea when things were going badly.

"Take the *lee*-wheel!" ordered Fegan.

"Ay, ay, sir," said Hurley crisply. He caught the wheel in its swing, and fell into position, hitching the lashing-rope about his body, bracing himself on wide feet against the agony-throes of the riotous craft.

I wanted to keep the lubber-line notched as steadily on the compass point as if the *Dovenby* were idling through the lazy Trades. Instead, in the wilder flurries, that black line swung incredibly—the ship took the bit in her teeth and ran away against a hard-over helm.

The ship's head whirled off the wind, dead against the ground-down helm—a spoke caught Hurley under the chin and almost broke his jaw!—and the main topsail went dead aback with a soul-shattering flap. The wind, previously on the beam, was now right aft; a terrific sea towered to the full height of the gaff-peak, halted as if licking its sinful lips in anticipation of ruin, then fell.

If I hadn't been wedged between box and wheel I should have been torn away and sluiced overboard, for in its transit that sea flattened the hurricane-rails of the lee-poop as if they were toffee-sticks. Hurley was carried to the extent of his lashing, which compressed his tough body so straitly that he coughed and doubled up inanimately. The foresail gave an unholy thump-thump and split in several places at once; that was all that saved the ship from total loss. For, with the wind-pressure eased for'ard, the helm came into effect; and though I hove up the spokes desperately to counter the wind'ard swing, the bow was definitely in the wind's eye before I had recovered my breath—jolted from my lungs by the excruciating impact of that great sea. I could see nothing of Captain Fegan. For once that wily man had been taken unawares. What I could see was that the cabin skylight was stove in like an eggshell, that the teakwood chart-house appeared to be shifted bodily from its moorings and was tilted at an odd angle to the vertical; that the whole for'ard poop-rail had gone, complete with bucket-racks, and that the waist was seethingly full of boiling foam.

The Struggle at the Wheel—III

As if to atone for her friskiness the ship was now tractable, answering every spoke of the wheel up or down; snorting along as if running before a vigorous north-east Trade. Hurley remained unconscious, doubled in his lashing like a half-empty sack in a sling. There was an awe-inspiring sense of loneliness everywhere. The fore-part of the ship, less than 200 feet from my position, holding practically all the crew, was as remote as if in the moon. Call as I might—in gasping intervals between tending the helm—no answer came. I wanted help to leeward; and, shaken to the core by that recent devastation, I wanted to be relieved, to spend a blissful minute under cover away from the merciless drive of the wind and the sledge-hammer blows of the boarding seas. My young soul started to panic.

But the reappearance of the skipper stiffened my wavering resolution. After all, he'd sent Hurley to the lee-wheel, which showed he had confidence in me; and the surest way to stiffen human confidence is to assure it that it is indomitable. When Fegan came crawling on hands and knees up the lee-poop-ladder I knew that I'd got to stick it out, just as he was doing. He was purple-faced, breathless; his oilskin slicker had been torn off him, and when he started to walk he limped awkwardly. He did not swear, was not even wrathful.

"I've broken my pipe!" was all the immediate comment he made. He straddled wide at the binnacle, looking aloft, then down into the bowl. The ship's nose was notched as if for ever exactly on its course.

"One day I'll make a helmsman of ye, young Shaw!" he commended. Then he started for'ard to ascertain the exact position there for himself. And the fury of the gale shut down again.

Fegan came back from his spluttering expedition and the very strong fore-topmast stay-sail was hauled up the stay; it helped to counteract the main topsail to some extent. "What's wrong with yon felly?" the captain asked, about Hurley, still limp in the holding-rope. He turned him over. I imagined the seaman to be dead. The blow of that sea should have sufficed to cut him in two; but he was alive—just.

"As if we weren't short-handed enough!" Fegan grumbled. But he carried Hurley into the chart-room, now dismantled, and handed him over to the bewildered steward.

As the ship lost her sea-kindliness again and began to fret on the helm, I had to appeal for a new hand to leeward. "Stick it out as well as ye can," said Fegan, and gave me a snifter of rum, which helped a lot. After that four-finger nip I felt capable of grinding the wheel off its spindle; but the effect died away after a while, leaving weariness.

Steering demanded too much concentrated attention to permit of much forward-looking, to see how the men progressed. With her freshened liveliness the ship took all my care, and the exertion, too, of all my strength. The wheel was never still—it was hard-up, hard-down incessantly. The number of times I was torn from my foothold and pitched half-way over the topmost spoke I dare not mention, for fear of disbelief. Such physical exercise is exhausting. One's joints feel wrenched apart. After sweating plentifully, the momentary lulls and easements caused the icy wind to cut like a knife, the wet clothes froze on the numbing body. It was an inward glow of triumph and power only that kept me warm in spots.

Then matters were adjusted for'ard; with supreme difficulty the newly bent fore-topsail was set; under its weight the ship picked up her giddy heels and ran amok. What speed she made during the next hour I cannot say; but she seemed irresistible—mad with demoniacal fury, determined to shake off the overwhelming impulse of that record storm. There were times when she leaned over so startlingly that I—Fegan, too—had the impression she would capsize; and, so heeled, she screamed through the seas like a run-away torpedo.

I had got the hang of her and she behaved with comparative docility. The new canvas steadied her to some extent; but it was as if a perfect understanding had been reached between ship and steersman. We each respected the other's strength and will. Tired as I was, the sense of unlimited power informed my every nerve. There are moments in human existence when the mortal man climbs to equality with the gods. If I felt secretly contemptuous of Fegan, Perkins and all hands, that was my own affair. I controlled the ship; she and I were one in harmony of intention.

"Send a hand to relieve the wheel!" ordered Fegan. "This man has been here fifteen hours." Someone whom I failed to identify in the inky darkness had taken the lee-wheel when the topsail was set and the ship in some degree cleared up. It was another old-timer who came to relieve. He took station behind me, gripped the spokes over my hands, and husked: "I'll take her, sundown!" I relinquished my control reluctantly. As soon as I was free of the responsibility weakness flooded over me.

But I wanted surcease from the everlasting drive of wind and sea. I thought to crawl down to the half-deck, and indulge in a smoke, a rub-down, dry clothing—if any were to be found. As I hesitated at the poop-break before descending into the swirl of the waist, the ship ran away from her helm. The newcomer had not realized what 15 hours' steady slogging had taught me—that the ship was alive and furious. She reeled over—over. She roared up into the full blast of the wind; and I had the impression of titanic, overwhelming power climbing high to wind'ard. Instinctively I leaped for the mizen-rigging and swarmed up, as high as time allowed. That gigantic wave crashed inboard. The ship vanished from view beneath a welter of ugly foam. She went dead. Things were fetching away aloft and on deck. The *Dovenby* was in her death-throes, so far as my instinct could make out.

I thought her going; but after a breathless eternity she shivered a little, fell back inert, shivered again, before hurling herself up to life. I heard my name called urgently.

"Get back to that wheel!" roared Fegan, when I replied. "The only man in the ship who can handle her, by all hell!" I went back, to stay until the next day grew out of night's screaming womb. They fed me and nourished me, when men went below to grapple with the shifted cargo by the light of smoky whale-oil lamps. They tended me like a Court favorite, and I nursed the *Dovenby* like any mother. Repeated attempts were made to give relief, but on each occasion the ship refused to be coaxed into subjection to another pair of hands. Each time I relinquished the weather spokes she behaved like a drunken slattern; each time I returned she calmed and gave reluctant obedience.

Twenty-eight hours of it, maybe more. Toward daylight the rumtots came frequently; but they lost their effect. There wasn't a prouder man afloat than I when I surrendered the spokes to a newcomer and staggered to my drenched bunk. Every effort had been worth while. In my young vanity I credited myself with saving that honest ship alive. Maybe I had.

Man Overboard!

The watch was up on the topsail-yard a-making fast the sail,
'N' Joe was swiggin' his gasket taut, 'n' I felt the stirrup give,
'N' he dropped sheer from the tops'l-yard 'n' barely cleared the rail,
'N' o' course, we bein' aloft, we couldn't do nothin' —
We couldn't lower a boat and go a-lookin' for him,
For it blew hard 'n' there was sech a sea runnin'
    That no boat wouldn't live.

I seed him rise in the white o' the wake, I seed him lift a hand
('N' him in his oilskin suit 'n' all), I heard him lift a cry;
'N' there was his place on the yard 'n' all, 'n' the stirrup's busted strand.
'N' the old man said, "There's a cruel old sea runnin',
A cold green Barney's Bull of a sea runnin';
It's hard, but I ain't agoin' to let a boat be lowered:"
    So we left him there to die.

He couldn't have kept afloat for long an' him lashed up 'n' all,
'N' we couldn't see him for long, for the sea was blurred with the sleet 'n' snow,
'N' we couldn't think of him much because o' the snortin', screamin' squall.
There was a hand less at the halliards 'n' the braces,
'N' a name less when the watch spoke to the muster-roll,
'N' a empty bunk 'n' a pannikin as wasn't wanted
    When the watch went below.

The Great Wandering Albatross

"Goneys and gullies an' all o' the birds o' the sea,
    They ain't no birds, not really," said Billy the Dane.
"Not mollies, nor gullies, nor goneys at all," said he,
    "But simply the sperrits of mariners livin' again.

"Them birds goin' fishin' is nothin' but souls o' the drowned,
    Souls of the drowned an' the kicked as are never no more;
An' that there haughty old albatross cruisin' around,
    Belike he's Admiral Nelson or Admiral Noah.

"An' merry's the life they are living. They settle and dip,
    They fishes, they never stands watches, they waggle their wings;
When a ship comes by, they fly to look at the ship
    To see how the nowaday mariners manages things.

"When freezing aloft in a snorter, I tell you I wish
    (Though maybe it ain't like a Christian)–I wish I could be
A haughty old copper-bound albatross dipping for fish
    And coming the proud over all o' the birds o' the sea."

Flying Fish Weather

I can never forget the eighteen or twenty days during which the light trade-winds were silently sweeping us towards the islands. All that we had to do, when our course was determined on, was to square in the yards and keep the vessel before the breeze, and then the good ship and the steady gale did the rest between them. The man at the wheel never vexed the old lady with any superfluous steering, but, comfortably adjusting his limbs at the tiller, would doze away by the hour. True to her work, the *Dolly* headed to her course, and, like one of those characters who always do best when let alone, she jogged on her way like a veteran old sea-pacer—as she was.

What a delightful, lazy, languid time we had whilst we were thus gliding along! There was nothing to be done; a circumstance that happily suited our disinclination to do anything. We abandoned the forepeak altogether, and spreading an awning over the forecastle, slept, ate, and lounged under it the livelong day. Every one seemed to be under the influence of some narcotic. Even the officers aft, whose duty required them never to be seated whilst keeping a deck watch, vainly endeavored to keep on their pins; and were obliged invariably to compromise the matter by leaning up against the bulwarks and gazing abstractedly over the side. Reading was out of the question; take a book in your hand, and you were asleep in an instant.

Although I could not avoid yielding in a great measure to the general languor, still at times I contrived to shake off the spell, and to appreciate the beauty of the scene around me. The sky presented a clear expanse of the most delicate blue, except along the skirts of the horizon, where you might see a thin drapery of pale clouds which never varied their form or color. The long, measured, dirge-like swell of the Pacific came rolling along, with its surface broken by little tiny waves, sparkling in the sunshine. Every now and then a shoal of flying-fish, scared from the water under the bows, would leap into the air, and fall the next moment like a shower of silver into the sea. Then you would see the superb albacore, with his glittering sides, sailing aloft, and, often describing an arc in his descent, disappear on the surface of the water. Far off, the lofty jet of the whale might be seen, and nearer at hand the prowling shark, that villainous footpad of the seas, would come skulking along, and, at a wary distance, regard us with his evil eye. At times some shapeless monster of the deep, floating on the surface, would, as we approached, sink slowly into the blue waters, and fade away from the sight. But the most impressive feature of the scene was the almost unbroken silence that reigned over sky and water. Scarcely a sound could be heard but the occasional breathing of the grampus and the rippling at the cutwater.

As we drew nearer the land, I hailed with delight the appearance of innumerable sea-fowl. Screaming and whirling in spiral tracks, they would accompany the vessel, and at times alight on our yards and stays. That piratical-looking fellow, appropriately named the man-of-war's hawk, with his blood-red bill and raven plumage, would come sweeping round us in gradually diminishing circles, till you could distinctly mark the strange flashings of his eye; and then, as if satisfied with his observation, would sail up into the air and disappear from the view. Soon, other evidences of our vicinity to the land were apparent, and it was not long before the glad announcement of its being in sight was heard from aloft—given with that peculiar prolongation of sound that a sailor loves—"Land ho!"

The captain, darting on deck from the cabin, bawled lustily for his spy-glass; the mate in still louder accents hailed the masthead with a tremendous "Where-away?" The black cook thrust his woolly head from the galley, and Boatswain, the dog, leaped up between the knightheads, and barked most furiously. Land ho! Aye, there it was. A hardly perceptible blue irregular outline, indicating the bold contour of the lofty heights of Nukuheva.

GORDON GRANT, ANTON OTTO FISCHER / HERMAN MELVILLE   195

Island Stop

The sloop's sails glow in the sun; the far sky burns,
Over the palm tree-tops wanders the dusk,
About the bows a chuckling ripple churns;
The land wind from the marshes smells of musk.
A star comes out; the moon is a pale husk;
Now, from the galley door, as supper nears,
Comes a sharp scent of meat and Spanish rusk
Fried in a pan. Far aft, where the lamp blears,
A seaman in a red shirt eyes the sails and steers.

Soon he will sight that isle in the dim bay
Where his mates saunter by the camp-fire's glow;
Soon will the birds scream, scared, and the bucks bray,
At the rattle and splash as the anchor is let go;
A block will pipe, and the oars grunt as they row,
He will meet his friends beneath the shadowy trees,
The moon's orb like a large lamp hanging low
Will see him stretched by the red blaze at ease,
Telling of the Indian girls, of ships, and of the seas.

Paradise Island

Oh, you'll never know Hawaii 'til you've kissed an Island girl
    And she's hung a ginger lei about your neck;
'Til you've danced the hula-hula on a beach of sand and pearl
    And have eaten opihis by the peck.

'Til you've hung your every garment on a big kamani tree
    And have felt the foaming surf about your knees;
'Til you've plunged into the breakers with a cry of pagan glee
    In a bathing suit of moonlight and a breeze.

'Til you've seen the lunar rainbow's phantom arch across the blue
    And have watched the Southern Cross dip in the sea;
'Til the singing boys have stabbed your heart with music . . . thru and thru;
    'Til you've raced the silver surf at Waikiki;

'Til you've slid down Ginger Jack . . . and every youngster knows the place;
    'Til you've gorged on pig until you couldn't think;
'Til you've seen the path of fury strewn with white-hot lava lace
    Where red Pele walks at Kilauea's brink.

'Til you've heard the old folks yarning of the days before today;
    At a luau over bowls of fish and poi;
'Til you've gone aboard a steamer with intent to stay away
    And have learned the meaning of "Aloha oe."

The Sea and the Land

Consider the subtleness of the sea; how its most dreaded creatures glide under water, unapparent for the most part, and treacherously hidden beneath the loveliest tints of azure. Consider also the devilish brilliance and beauty of many of its most remorseless tribes, as the dainty embellished shape of many species of sharks. Consider, once more, the universal cannibalism of the sea; all whose creatures prey upon each other, carrying on eternal war since the world began.

Consider all this; and then turn to this green, gentle, and most docile earth; consider them both, the sea and the land; and do you not find a strange analogy to something in yourself? For as this appalling ocean surrounds the verdant land, so in the soul of man there lies one insular Tahiti, full of peace and joy, but encompassed by all the horrors of the half-known life. God keep thee! Push not off from that isle, thou canst never return!

201

We're Homeward Bound

We're home-ward bound,— I hear— them say, Good-
bye, fare you well,—good-bye, fare you well, We're home-ward bound, I
hear— them say, Hur-rah! my boys, we're home-ward bound.

We're homeward bound this very day,
    Goodbye, fare you well, goodbye, fare you well,
We're homeward bound this very day,
    Hurrah! my boys, we're homeward bound.

We're homeward bound for 'Frisco town,
    Goodbye, fare you well, goodbye, fare you well,
We're homeward bound for 'Frisco town,
    Hurrah! my boys, we're homeward bound.

Oh, heave away, she's up and down.

Those 'Frisco girls, they've got us in tow.

And it's goodbye to Katie and goodnight to Nell.

Oh, it's goodbye again and fare you well.

And now I hear our first mate say.

Her anchor, boys, we soon will see.

We're homeward bound, 'tis a joyous sound.

I thought I heard our old man say,
    Goodbye, fare you well, goodbye, fare you well,
I thought I heard our old man say,
    Hurrah! my boys, we're homeward bound.

Oh, 'Frisco Bay in three months and a day,
    Goodbye, fare you well, goodbye, fare you well,
Oh, 'Frisco Bay in three months and a day,
    Hurrah! my boys, we're homeward bound.

We've got the fluke at last in sight,
    Goodbye, fare you well, goodbye, fare you well,
We've got the fluke at last in sight,
    Hurrah! my boys, we're homeward bound.
        'VAST HEAVING!

Jack's Battle Yarn

Among innumerable "*yarns and twisters*" reeled off in our main-top during our pleasant run to the North, none could match those of Jack Chase.

Never was there better company than ever-glorious Jack. The things which most men only read of, or dream about, he had seen and experienced. He had been a dashing smuggler in his day, and could tell of a long nine-pounder rammed home with wads of French silks; of cartridges stuffed with the finest gunpowder tea; of cannister-shot full of West Indian sweetmeats; of sailor frocks and trowsers, quilted inside with costly laces; and table legs, hollow as musket barrels, compactly stowed with rare drugs and spices. He could tell of a wicked widow, too—a beautiful receiver of smuggled goods upon the English coast—who smiled so sweetly upon the smugglers when they sold her silks and laces, cheap as tape and ginghams. She called them gallant fellows, hearts of game; and bade them bring her more.

He could tell of desperate fights with his British majesty's cutters, in midnight coves upon a stormy coast; of the capture of a reckless band, and their being drafted on board a man-of-war; of their swearing that their chief was slain; of a writ of habeas corpus sent on board for one of them for a debt—a reserved and handsome man—and his going ashore, strongly suspected of being the slaughtered captain, and this a successful scheme for his escape.

But more than all, Jack could tell of the battle of Navarino, for he had been a captain of one of the main-deck guns on board Admiral Codrington's flag-ship, the Asia. Were mine the style of stout old Chapman's Homer, even then I would scarce venture to give noble Jack's own version of this fight, wherein, on the 20th of October, A.D. 1827, thirty-two sail of Englishmen, Frenchmen, and Russians, attacked and vanquished in the Levant an Ottoman fleet of three ships-of-the-line, twenty-five frigates, and a swarm of fire ships and hornet craft.

"We bayed to be at them," said Jack; "and when we *did* open fire, we were like dolphin among the flying-fish. 'Every man take his bird' was the cry, when we trained our guns. And those guns all smoked like rows of Dutch pipe-bowls, my hearties! My gun's crew carried small flags in their bosoms, to nail to the mast in case the ship's colors were shot away. Stripped to the waistbands, we fought like skinned tigers, and bowled down the Turkish frigates like nine-pins. Among their shrouds—swarming thick with small-arm men, like flights of pigeons lighted on pine-trees—our marines sent their leaden pease and gooseberries, like a shower of hail-stones in Labrador. It was a stormy time, my hearties! The blasted Turks pitched into the old Asia's hull a whole quarry of marble shot, each ball one hundred and fifty pounds. They knocked three port-holes into one. But we gave them better than they sent. 'Up and at them, my bull-dog!' said I, patting my gun on the breech; 'tear open hatchways in their Moslem sides!' White-Jacket, my lad, you ought to have been there. The bay was covered with masts and yards, as I have seen a raft of snags in the Arkansas River. Showers of burned rice and olives from the exploding foe fell upon us like manna in the wilderness. '*Allah! Allah! Mohammed! Mohammed!*' split the air; some cried it out from the Turkish port-holes; others shrieked it forth from the drowning waters, their top-knots floating on their shaven skulls, like black-snakes on half-tide rocks. By those top-knots they believed that their Prophet would drag them up to Paradise, but they sank fifty fathoms, my hearties, to the bottom of the bay. 'Ain't the bloody 'Hometons going to strike yet?' cried my first loader, a Guernsey man, thrusting his neck out of the port-hole, and looking at the Turkish line-of-battle ship near by. That instant his head blew by me like a bursting Paixhan shot, and the flag of Ned Knowles himself was hauled down forever. We dragged his hull to one side, and avenged him with the cooper's anvil, which, endways, we rammed home; a mess-mate shoved in the dead man's bloody Scotch cap for the wad, and sent it flying into the line-of-battle ship. By the god of war! boys, we hardly left enough of that craft to boil a pot of water with. It was a hard day's work—a sad day's work, my hearties. That night, when all was over, I slept sound enough, with a box of cannister shot for my pillow!"

"But how did you feel, Jack, when the musket-ball carried away one of your hooks there?"

"Feel! only a finger the lighter. I have seven more left, besides thumbs; and they did good service, too, in the torn rigging the day after the fight; for you must know, my hearties, that the hardest work comes after the guns are run in. Three days I helped work, with one hand, in the rigging, in the same trowsers that I wore in the action; the blood had dried and stiffened; they looked like glazed red morocco."

Yet this Jack Chase had a heart in him like a mastodon's. I have seen him weep when a man was flogged at the gangway.

The Passing Ship

I was at sea in a sailing ship, walking up and down the lee side of the poop, keeping the time, and striking the bell at each half-hour. It was early in the morning watch, a little after four in the morning. We were in the tropics, not very far from the Doldrums, in the last of the Trades. We were sailing slowly, making perhaps some three or four knots an hour under all sail. The dawn was in the sky to leeward of us, full of wonderful colour, full of embers and fire, changing the heaven, smouldering and burning, breaking out in bloody patches, fading into faint gold, into grey, into a darkness like smoke. There was a haze on the sea, very white and light, moving and settling. Dew was dripping from the sails, from the ropes, from the eaves of the charthouse. The decks shone with dew. In the half-light of the dusk, the binnacle lamps burnt pale and strangely. There was a red patch forward, in the water and on the mist, where the sidelight burned. The men were moving to and fro on the deck below me, walking slowly in couples, one of them singing softly, others quietly talking. They had not settled down to sleep since the muster, because they were expecting the morning "coffee," then brewing in the galley. The galley funnel sent trails of sparks over to leeward, and now and then the cook passed to the ship's side to empty ashes into the sea. It was a scene common enough. The same pageant was played before me every other day, whenever I had the morning watch. There was the sunrise and the dewy decks, the sails dripping, and the men shuffling about along the deck. But on this particular day the common scenes and events were charged with meaning as though they were the initiation to a mystery, the music playing before a pageant. It may have been the mist, which made everything unreal and uncertain, especially in the twilight, with the strange glow coming through it from the dawn. I remember that a block made a soft melancholy piping noise in the mizzen rigging as though a bird had awakened upon a branch, and the noise, though common enough, made everything beautiful, just as a little touch of colour will set off a sombre picture and give a value to each tint. Then the ball of the sun came out of the sea in a mass of blood and fire, spreading streamers of gold and rose along the edges of the clouds to the mid-heaven. As he climbed from the water, and the last stars paled, the haze lifted and died. Its last shadows moved away from the sea like grey deer going to new pasture, and as they went, the look-out gave a hail of a ship being to windward of us.

When I saw her first there was a smoke of mist about her as high as her foreyard. Her topsails and flying kites had a faint glow upon them where the dawn caught them. Then the mist rolled away from her, so that we could see her hull and the glimmer of the red sidelight as it was hoisted inboard. She was rolling slightly, tracing an arc against the heaven, and as I watched her the glow upon her deepened, till every sail she wore burned rosily like an opal turned to the sun, like a fiery jewel. She was radiant, she was of an immortal beauty, that swaying, delicate clipper. Coming as she came, out of the mist into the dawn, she was like a spirit, like an intellectual presence. Her hull glowed, her rails glowed; there was colour upon the boats and tackling. She was a lofty ship (with skysails and royal staysails), and it was wonderful to watch her, blushing in the sun, swaying and curveting. She was alive with a more than mortal life. One thought that she would speak in some strange language or break out into a music which would express the sea and that great flower in the sky. She came trembling down to us, rising up high and plunging; showing the red lead below her water-line; then diving down till the smother bubbled over her hawseholes. She bowed and curveted; the light caught the skylights on the poop; she gleamed and sparkled; she shook the sea from her as she rose. There was no man aboard of us but was filled with the beauty of that ship. I think they would have cheered her had she been a little nearer to us; but, as it was, we ran up our flags in answer to her, adding our position and comparing our chronometers, then dipping our ensigns and standing away. For some minutes I watched her, as I made up the flags before putting them back in their cupboard. The old mate limped up to me, and spat and swore. "That's one of the beautiful sights of the world," he said. "That, and a cornfield, and a woman with her child. It's beauty and strength. How would you like to have one of them skysails round her neck?" I gave him some answer, and continued to watch her, till the beautiful, precise hull, with all its lovely detail, had become blurred to leeward, where the sun was now marching in triumph, the helm of a golden warrior plumed in cirrus.

Burial at Sea

Blue gulf all around us,
    Blue sky overhead—
Muster all on the quarter,
    We must bury the dead!

It is but a Danish sailor,
    Rugged of front and form;
A common son of the forecastle,
    Grizzled with sun and storm.

His name, and the strand he hailed from
    We know, and there's nothing more!
But perhaps his mother is waiting
    In the lonely Island of Fohr.

Still, as he lay there dying,
    Reason drifting awreck,
"'Tis my watch," he would mutter,
    "I must go upon deck!"

Aye, on deck, by the foremast!
    But watch and lookout are done;
The Union Jack laid o'er him,
    How quiet he lies in the sun!

Slow the ponderous engine,
    Stay the hurrying shaft;
Let the roll of the ocean
    Cradle our giant craft;
Gather around the grating,
    Carry your messmate aft!

Stand in order, and listen
    To the holiest page of prayer.
Let every foot be quiet,
    Every head be bare—
The soft trade-wind is lifting
    A hundred locks of hair.

Our captain reads the service,
    (A little spray on his cheeks)
The grand old words of burial,
    And the trust a true heart seeks:—
"We therefore commit his body
    To the deep"—and, as he speaks,

Launched from the weather railing,
    Swift as the eye can mark,
The ghastly, shotted hammock
    Plunges, away from the shark,
Down, a thousand fathoms,
    Down into the dark!

A thousand summers and winters
    The stormy Gulf shall roll
High o'er his canvas coffin;
    But, silence to doubt and dole:—
There's a quiet harbor somewhere
    For the poor aweary soul.

Free the fettered engine,
    Speed the tireless shaft,
Loose to'gallant and topsail,
    The breeze is fair abaft!

Blue sea all around us,
    Blue sky bright o'erhead—
Every man to his duty,
    We have buried our dead!

Bert's Yarn

He lolled on a bollard, a sun-burned son of the sea,
With ear-rings of brass and a jumper of dungaree,
"'N' many a queer lash-up have I seen," says he.

"But the toughest horray o' the racket," he says, "I'll be sworn,
'N' the roughest traverse I worked since the day I was born,
Was a packet o' Sailor's Delight as I scoffed in the seas o' the Horn.

"All day long in the calm she had rolled to the swell,
Rolling through fifty degrees till she clattered her bell;
'N' then came snow, 'n' a squall, 'n' a wind was colder 'n hell.

"It blew like the Bull of Barney, a beast of a breeze,
'N' over the rail come the cold green lollopin' seas,
'N' she went ashore at the dawn on the Ramirez.

"She was settlin' down by the stern when I got to the deck,
Her waist was a smother o' sea as was up to your neck,
'N' her masts were gone, 'n' her rails, 'n' she was a wreck.

"We rigged up a tackle, a purchase, a sort of a shift,
To hoist the boats off o' the deck-house and get them adrift,
When her stern gives a sickenin' settle, her bows give a lift,

"'N' comes a crash of green water as sets me afloat
With freezing fingers clutching the keel of a boat—
The bottom-up whaler—'n' that was the juice of a note.

"Well, I clambers acrost o' the keel 'n' I gets me secured,
When I sees a face in the white o' the smother to looard,
So I gives 'im a 'and, 'n' be shot if it wasn't the stooard!

"So he climbs up forrard o' me, 'n' 'thanky,' a' says,
'N' we sits 'n' shivers 'n' freeze to the bone wi' the sprays,
'N' I sings 'Abel Brown,' 'n' the stooard he prays.

"Wi' never a dollop to sup nor a morsel to bite,
The lips of us blue with the cold 'n' the heads of us light,
Adrift in a Cape Horn sea for a day 'n' a night.

"'N' then the stooard goes dotty 'n' puts a tune to his lip,
'N' moans about Love like a dern old hen wi' the pip—
(I sets no store upon stooards—they ain't no use on a ship).

"'N' 'mother,' the looney cackles, 'come 'n' put Willy to bed!'
So I says 'Dry up, or I'll fetch you a crack o' the head';
'The kettle's a-bilin',' he answers, ''n' I'll go butter the bread.'

"'N' he falls to singin' some slush about clinkin' a can,
'N' at last he dies, so he does, 'n' I tells you, Jan,
I was glad when he did, for he weren't no fun for a man.

"So he falls forrard, he does, 'n' he closes his eye,
'N' quiet he lays 'n' quiet I leaves him lie,
'N' I was alone with his corp, 'n' the cold green sea and the sky.

"'N' then I dithers, I guess, for the next as I knew
Was the voice of a mate as was sayin' to one of the crew,
'Easy, my son, wi' the brandy, be shot if he ain't comin'-to!'"

Iceberg

At twelve o'clock we went below, and had just got through dinner, when the cook put his head down the scuttle and told us to come on deck and see the finest sight we had ever seen. "Where away, cook?" asked the first man who was up. "On the larboard bow." And there lay, floating on the ocean, several miles off, an immense, irregular mass, its top and points covered with snow, and its centre of a deep indigo colour. This was an iceberg, and of the largest size, as one of our men said who had been in the Northern Ocean. As far as the eye could reach, the sea in every direction was of a deep blue colour, the waves running high and fresh, and sparkling in the light, and in the midst lay this immense mountain-island, its cavities and valleys thrown into deep shade, and its points and pinnacles glittering in the sun. All hands were soon on deck, looking at it, and admiring in various ways its beauty and grandeur. But no description can give any idea of the strangeness, splendour, and really, the sublimity of the sight. Its great size—for it must have been two to three miles in circumference and several hundred feet in height;—its slow motion, as its base rose and sank in the water, and its high points nodded against the clouds; the dashing of the waves upon it, which, breaking high with foam, lined its base with a white crust; and the thundering sound of the cracking of the mass, and the breaking and tumbling down of huge pieces; together with its nearness and approach, which added a slight element of fear,—all combined to give to it the character of true sublimity. The main body of the mass was, as I have said, of an indigo colour, its base crusted with frozen foam; and as it grew thin and transparent towards the edges and top, its colour shaded off from a deep blue to the whiteness of snow. It seemed to be drifting slowly towards the north, so that we kept away and avoided it. It was in sight all the afternoon; and when we got to the leeward of it, the wind died away, so that we lay-to quite near it for the greater part of the night. Unfortunately, there was no moon, but it was a clear night, and we could plainly mark the long, regular heaving of the stupendous mass, as its edges moved slowly against the stars. Several times on our watch loud cracks were heard, which sounded as though they must have run through the whole length of the iceberg, and several pieces fell down with a thundering crash, plunging heavily into the sea. Towards morning, a strong breeze sprang up, and we filled away, and left it astern, and at daylight it was out of sight.

Fog

Thick weather! The horizon closed to us at a length or so ahead. But she was moving slowly, four knots at the most, and we were well out of the track of ships! Oh, it was all right—all right; and aft there the Mate leaned over the poop rail with his arms squared and his head nodding—now and then!

As the light grew, it seemed to bring intenser cold. Jackets were not enough; we donned coats and oil-skins and stamped and stamped on the foredeck, yawning and muttering and wishing it was five o'clock and the 'doctor' ready with the blessèd coffee: the coffee that would make men of us; vile 'hogwash' that a convict would turn his face at, but what seemed nectar to us at daybreak, down there in fifty-five!

By one bell the mist had grown denser, and the Mate sung out sudden and angrily for the foghorn to be sounded.

"Three blasts, d'ye 'ear," said the bo'sun, passing the horn up to Dago, the look-out. "Uno! . . . Doo! . . . Tray!" (Three fingers held up.) . . . "Tray, ye burnt scorpion! . . . An' see that ye sounds 'em proper, or I'll come up there an' hide the soul-case out o' ye! . . . (Cowpunchin' hoodlum! Good job I knows *is* bloomin' lingo!)"

Now we had a tune to our early rising, a doleful tune, a tune set to the deepening mist, the heaving sea, at dismal break of day. *R-r-ah! . . . R-r-ah! . . . Ra!* was the way it ran; a mournful bar, with windy gasps here and there, for Dago Joe was more accustomed to a cowhorn.

"A horn," said Welsh John suddenly. "Did 'oo hear it?"

No one had heard. We were gathered round the galley door, all talking, all telling the 'doctor' the best way to light a fire quickly.

"Iss! A horn, I tell 'oo! . . . Listen! . . . Just after ours is sounded!"

R-r-ah! . . . R-r-ah! . . . R-ah! Joe was improving.

We listened intently. . . . "There now," said John!

Yes! Sure enough! Faint rasps answering ours. Ulrichs said three; two, I thought!

"Don't ye 'ear that 'orn, ye dago fiddler," shouted the bo'sun.

. . . "'Ere! Hup there, one of ye, an' blow a proper blast! That damn hoodlum! Ye couldn't 'ear 'is trumpetin' at th' back of an area railin's!"

John went on the head; the bo'sun aft to report.

A proper blast! The Welshman had the trick of the wheezing 'gadjet'. . . . Ah! There again! . . . Three blasts, right enough! . . . She would be a square rigger, running, like ourselves! . . . Perhaps we were making on her! . . . The sound seemed louder. . . . It came from ahead!

R-R-R-R-R-AH! . . . R-R-R-R-R-AH! . . . R-R-R-R-R-AH! . . . *R-r-r-r-eh! . . . R-r-r-r-eh! . . . R-r-r-r-eh!*

The Mate was now on the alert, peering and listening. At the plain answer to our horn, he rapped out orders. "Lower away main an' fore-to'gal'ns'ls . . . let 'em hang, an' lay aft and haul th' mains'l up! Come aft here, one of you boys, and call th' Captain! Tell him it's come down thick! Sharp, now!"

I went below and roused the Old Man.

"Aye . . . all right," he said, feeling for his seaboots. (South'ard of the 'forties' Old Jock slept 'all standing,' as we say.) "Thick, eh? . . . Tell th' Mate t' keep th' horn goin'! . . . A ship, ye say? . . . Running, eh? . . . Aye! All right. . . . I'll be up. . . ."

I had scarcely reached the poop again before the Old Man was at my back.

"Thick, b' Goad," he said, rubbing his eyes. "Man, man! Why was I not called before?"

The Mate muttered something about the mist having just closed in. . . . "Clear enough t' be goin' on before that," he said.

"Aye, aye! Where d'ye mak' this ship? Ye would see her before the mist cam' doon, eh?"

"Sound that horn, forrard there," shouted the Mate, moving off to the gangway! "Keep that horn going, there!" John pumped a stirring blast. . . . R-R-R-R-R-AH! R-R-R-R-R-AH! . . . R-R-R-R-R-AH!

We bent forward with ears strained to catch the distant note.

. . . *R-r-r-r-eh!* . . . At the first answering blast Old Jock raised his head, glancing fearfully round.

. . . *R-r-r-r-eh! . . . R-r-r-r*—"Down hellum! Down HELLUM! DOWN," he yelled, running aft to the wheel! "Haul yards forrard! Le'go port braces! Let 'm rip! Le'go an' haul! . . . Quick, Mist'r! Christ! What ye standin' at? . . . Ice! Ice, ye bluidy eedi't! Ice! Th' echo! Let go! LE'GO AN' HAUL! LE'GO!"

Fog and Ice-1

Ice! The Mate stood stupid for an instant—then jumped to the waist—to the brace pins—roaring hoarse orders. "All hands on deck! Haul away, there! All hands! On deck, men—for your lives!"

Ice! At the dread cry we ran to the ropes and tailed on with desperate energy! Ice! The watch below, part dressed, swarmed from house and fo'cas'le and hauled with us—a light of terror in their eyes—the terror that comes with stark reason—when the brain reels from restful stupor at a trumpet of alarms!

Ice! The decks, that so late had been quiet as the air about us, resounded to the din of sudden action! Yards swinging forward with a crash—blocks *whirring*—ropes hurtling from the pins—sails lifting and thrashing to the masts—shouts and cries from the swaying haulers at the ropes—hurried orders—and, loud over all, the raucous bellow of the foghorn when Dago Joe, dismayed at the confusion, pumped furiously, *Ra! Ra! Ra! Ra! Ra!*

. . . *Reh! Reh! Reh! Reh! Reh!* . . . Note for note—the echo—out of the mist!

"Belay, all! Well, mainyards!" The order steadied us. We had time now to look! . . . There was nothing in sight! . . . No towering monster looming in our path—no breakers—no sea—no sky; nothing! Nothing but the misty wall that veiled our danger! The Unknown! The Unseen!

She was swinging slowly against the scend of the running swell—laying up to the wind. Martin had the wheel and was holding the helm down, his keen eyes watching for the lift that would mark the limit of steering-way. The old man stood by the compass, bending, peering, sniffing—nosing at the keen air—his quick eyes searching the mist—ahead—abeam—astern. . . . Martin eased the helm, she lay quietly with sails edged to the wind, the long swell heaving at her—broadside on.

Suddenly a light grew out of the mist and spread out on both bows—a luminous sheen, low down on the narrowed sea-line! The 'ice-blink'! Cold! White!

At the first glow the Old Man started—his lips framed to roar an order! . . . No order came.

Quickly he saw the hopelessness of it; what was to happen was plain, inevitable! Broad along the beam, stretching out to leeward, the great dazzling 'ice-blink' warned him of a solid barrier, miles long, perhaps! The barque lay to the wind, at mercy of the swell, drifting dead to leeward at every heave! . . . On the other tack, perhaps? There was a misty gap to the south of us; no 'ice-blink' there! . . . If she could be put about? . . . No, there was no chance! . . . To gather speed to put her about he would have to bear off towards the brightening sheen! Already the roar of the swell, lashing at the base, was loud in our ears! . . . There was no room! No sea-room to wear or stay!

"Embayed!" he said bitterly, turning his palms up! . . . "All hands aft and swing th' port boat out!"

The port boat? The big boat? Had it come, so soon, to that? More than one of us cast an anxious look at the broad figure of our Master as we ran aft. He stood quite still, glaring out at the ice ring.

"This is it, eh!" he muttered, unheeding the stir and cries of us. "This is it—after forty year!"

Madly we tore and knifed at the lashings, working to clear the big boat. She was turned down on the skids (the fashion of thrifty 'limejuicers'), bound and bolted to stand the heavy weather. We were handless, unnerved by the suddenness of it all, faulty at the task. The roar of breaking water spurred us on. . . . A heave together! . . . Righted, we hooked the falls and swayed her up. The Mate looked aft for the word. "Aye," said the Old Man, "oot wi' her, an' try tae tow th' heid roun'! On th' ither tack we micht——" He left the words unfinished! Well he knew we could never drag three thousand tons against that swell.

A wild outcry turned our eyes forward. Dago Joe (forgotten on the look-out) is running aft, his precious horn still slung from his shoulders. "*Arretto! Arretto! Arretto!*" He yells as he runs. "*Arretto, Capitan!*" waving his arms and signing to the Old Man to stop the ship! Behind him, over the bows, we see the clear outline of a small berg—an outflung 'calf' of the main ice! There is no time! Nothing can be done! Small as the berg is—not the height of our lower yards—it has weight enough to sink us, when aided by the heaving swell!

"Quick with th' boat, there," yells the Old Man! He runs over to the companion-way and dives below, jostling the Second Mate, who is staggering up under a weight of biscuit bags.

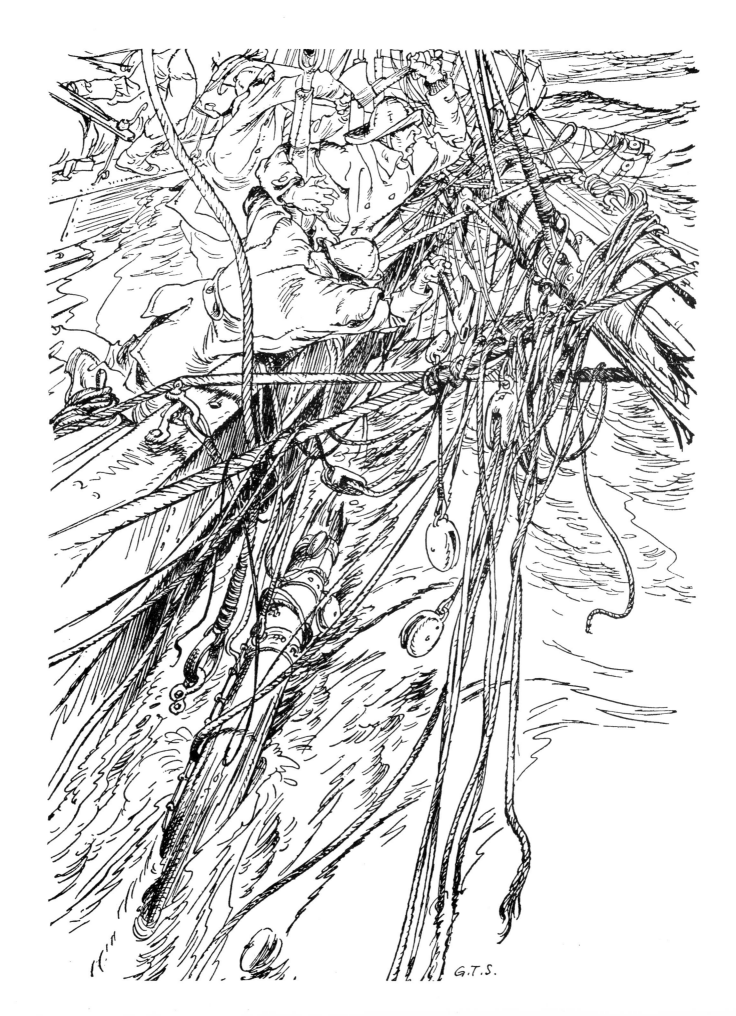

Fog and Ice – II

In a moment we have closed with the ice and are hammering and grinding at the sheer glistening wall. At the first impact the boom goes with a crash! Then fore-to' gallant mast—yards—sails—rigging all hurtling to the head, driving the decks in! A shelf of solid ice, tons weight of it, crashes aboard and shatters the fore-hatch! Now there is a grind and scream of buckling iron, as the beams give to the strain—ring of stays and guy-ropes, parting at high tension—crash of splintering wood! The heaving monster draws off, reels, and comes at us again! Another blow and——

"'Vast lowering! Hold on! Hold on the boat there!" The Old Man, come on deck with his treasured papers, has seen more than the wreck of the head! He runs to the compass—a look—then casts his eyes aloft. "Square mainyards!" His voice has the old confident ring: the ring we know. "Square mainyards! . . . A hand t' th' wheel!"

Doubting, we hang around the boat. She swings clear, all ready? The jar of a further blow sets us staggering for foothold! What chance? . . . "A hand t' th' wheel, here," roars the Old Man. Martin looks up . . . he goes back to his post.

A man at the wheel again! No longer the fearful sight of the main post deserted; no longer the jar and rattle of a handless helm!

Martin's action steadies us. What dread, when the oldest of us all stands there grasping the spokes, waiting the order? . . . We leave the swinging boat and hurry to the braces!

A 'chance' has come! The power of gales long since blown out is working a way for us; the ghostly descendants of towering Cape Horn 'greybeards' have come to our aid!

As we struck, sidling on the bows, the swell has swept our stern round the berg. Now we are head to wind and the big foresail is flat against the mast, straining sternward!

It is broad day, and we see the 'calf' plainly as we drift under stern-way apart. The gap widens! A foot—a yard—an oar's length! Now the wind stirs the canvas on the main—a clew lifts—the tops'ls rustle and blow out, drawing finely! Her head still swings!

"Foreyards! Le'go an' haul!" roars the Old Man. We are stern on to the main ice. Already the swell—recurving from the sheer base—is hissing and breaking about us. There is little room for stern-board. "Le'go an' haul!" We roar a heartening chorus as we drag the standing headyards in.

Slowly she brings up . . . gathers way . . . moves ahead! The 'calf' is dead to windward, the loom of the main ice astern and a-lee. The wind has strengthened: in parts the mist has cleared. Out to the south'ard a lift shows clear water. We are broad to the swell now, but sailing free as Martin keeps her off! From under the bows the broken boom (still tethered to us by stout guy-ropes) thunders and jars as we move through the water.

"Cut and clear away!" roars Old Jock. "Let her go!"

Aye, let her go! . . . We are off . . . crippled an' all . . . out for open sea again!

NORMAN WILKINSON / JOSEPH CONRAD

The Implacable Sea

. . . The sea has never been friendly to man. At most it has been the accomplice of human restlessness, and playing the part of dangerous abettor of world-wide ambitions. Faithful to no race after the manner of the kindly earth, receiving no impress from valour and toil and self-sacrifice, recognizing no finality of dominion, the sea has never adopted the cause of its masters like those lands where the victorious nations of mankind have taken root, rocking their cradles and setting up their gravestones. He—man or people—who, putting his trust in the friendship of the sea, neglects the strength and cunning of his right hand, is a fool! As if it were too great, too mighty for common virtues, the ocean has no compassion, no faith, no law, no memory. Its fickleness is to be held true to men's purposes only by an undaunted resolution and by a sleepless, armed, jealous vigilance, in which, perhaps, there has always been more hate than love. *Odi et amo* may well be the confession of those who consciously or blindly have surrendered their existence to the fascination of the sea. All the tempestuous passions of mankind's young days, the love of loot and the love of glory, the love of adventure and the love of danger, with the great love of the unknown and vast dreams of dominion and power, have passed like images reflected from a mirror, leaving no record upon the mysterious face of the sea. Impenetrable and heartless, the sea has given nothing of itself to the suitors for its precarious favours. Unlike the earth, it cannot be subjugated at any cost of patience and toil. For all its fascination that has lured so many to a violent death, its immensity has never been loved as the mountains, the plains, the desert itself, have been loved.

Singleton, at the wheel, yelled out: "Look out for yourselves!" His voice reached them in a warning whisper. They were startled.

A big, foaming sea came out of the mist; it made for the ship, roaring wildly, and in its rush it looked as mischievous and discomposing as a madman with an axe. One or two, shouting, scrambled up the rigging; most, with a convulsive catch of the breath, held on where they stood. Singleton dug his knees under the wheel box, and carefully eased the helm to the headlong pitch of the ship, but without taking his eyes off the coming wave. It towered close-to and high, like a wall of green glass topped with snow. The ship rose to it as though she had soared on wings, and for a moment rested poised upon the foaming crest as if she had been a great sea bird. Before we could draw breath a heavy gust struck her, another roller took her unfairly under the weather bow, she gave a toppling lurch, and filled her decks. Captain Allistoun leaped up, and fell; Archie rolled over him, screaming: "She will rise!" She gave another lurch to leeward; the lower deadeyes dipped heavily; the men's feet flew from under them, and they hung kicking above the slanting poop. They could see the ship putting her side in the water, and shouted all together: "She's going!" Forward the forecastle doors flew open, and the watch below were seen leaping out one after another, throwing their arms up; and, falling on hands and knees, scrambled aft on all fours along the high side of the deck, sloping more than the roof of a house. From leeward the seas rose, pursuing them; they looked wretched in a hopeless struggle, like vermin fleeing before a flood; they fought up the weather ladder of the poop one after another, half naked and staring wildly; and as soon as they got up they shot to leeward in clusters, with closed eyes, till they brought up heavily with their ribs against the iron stanchions of the rail; then, groaning, they rolled in a confused mass. The immense volume of water thrown forward by the last scend of the ship had burst the lee door of the forecastle. They could see their chests, pillows, blankets, clothing, come out floating upon the sea. While they struggled back to windward they looked in dismay. The straw beds swam high, the blankets, spread out, undulated; while the chests, waterlogged and with a heavy list, pitched heavily, like dismasted hulks, before they sank; Archie's big coat passed with outspread arms, resembling a drowned seaman floating with his head under water.

Knocked Down-1

Knocked Down-II

Men were slipping down while trying to dig their fingers into the planks; others, jammed in corners, rolled enormous eyes. They all yelled unceasingly: "The masts! Cut! Cut! . . ." A black squall howled low over the ship, that lay on her side with the weather yardarms pointing to the clouds; while the tall masts, inclined nearly to the horizon, seemed to be of an unmeasurable length. The carpenter let go his hold, rolled against the skylight, and began to crawl to the cabin entrance, where a big axe was kept ready for just such an emergency. At that moment the topsail sheet parted, the end of the heavy chain racketed aloft, and sparks of red fire streamed down through the flying sprays. The sail flapped once with a jerk that seemed to tear our hearts out through our teeth, and instantly changed into a bunch of fluttering narrow ribbons that tied themselves into knots and became quiet along the yard. Captain Allistoun struggled, managed to stand up with his face near the deck, upon which men swung on the ends of ropes, like nest robbers upon a cliff. One of his feet was on somebody's chest; his face was purple; his lips moved. He yelled

also; he yelled, bending down: "No! No!" Mr. Baker, one leg over the binnacle-stand, roared out: "Did you say no? Not cut?" He shook his head madly. "No! No!" Between his legs the crawling carpenter heard, collapsed at once, and lay full length in the angle of the skylight. Voices took up the shout—"No! No!" Then all became still. They waited for the ship to turn over altogether, and shake them out into the sea; and upon the terrific noise of wind and sea not a murmur of remonstrance came out from those men, who each would have given ever so many years of life to see "them damned sticks go overboard!" They all believed it their only chance; but a little hard-faced man shook his gray head and shouted "No!" without giving them as much as a glance. They were silent, and gasped. They gripped rails, they had wound ropes'-ends under their arms; they clutched ringbolts, they crawled in heaps where there was foothold; they held on with both arms, hooked themselves to anything to windward with elbows, with chins, almost with their teeth; and some, unable to crawl away from where they had been flung, felt the sea leap up, striking against their backs as they struggled upwards. Singleton had stuck to the wheel. His hair flew out in the wind; the gale seemed to take its life-long adversary by the beard and shake his old head. He wouldn't let go, and, with his knees forced between the spokes, flew up and down like a man on a bough. As Death appeared unready, they began to look about. Donkin, caught by one foot in a loop of some rope, hung, head down, below us, and yelled, with his face to the deck: "Cut! Cut!" Two men lowered themselves cautiously to him; others hauled on the rope. They caught him up, shoved him into a safer place, held him. He shouted curses at the master, shook his fist at him with horrible blasphemies, called upon us in filthy words to "Cut! Don't mind that murdering fool! Cut, some of you!" One of his rescuers struck him a backhanded blow over the mouth; his head banged on the deck, and he became suddenly very quiet, with a white face, breathing hard, and with a few drops of blood trickling from his cut lip. . . . Mr. Baker crawled along the line of men, asking: "Are you all there?" and looking them over. Some blinked vacantly, others shook convulsively; Wamibo's head hung over his breast; and in painful attitudes, cut by lashings, exhausted with clutching, screwed up in corners, they breathed heavily. Their lips twitched, and at every sickening heave of the overturned ship they opened them wide as if to shout. The cook, embracing a wooden stanchion, unconsciously repeated a prayer. In every short interval of the fiendish noises around he could be heard there, without cap or slippers, imploring in that storm the Master of our lives not to lead him into temptation. Soon he also became silent. In all that crowd of cold and hungry men, waiting wearily for a violent death, not a voice was heard; they were mute, and in somber thoughtfulness listened to the horrible imprecations of the gale.

Hours passed. They were sheltered by the heavy inclination of the ship from the wind that rushed in one long unbroken moan above their heads, but cold rain showers fell at times into the uneasy calm of their refuge. Under the torment of that new infliction a pair of shoulders would writhe a little. Teeth chattered. The sky was clearing, and bright sunshine gleamed over the ship. After every burst of battering seas, vivid and fleeting rainbows arched over the drifting hull in the flick of sprays. The gale was ending in a clear blow, which gleamed and cut like a knife. Between two bearded shellbacks Charley, fastened with somebody's long muffler to a deck ringbolt, wept quietly, with rare tears wrung out by bewilderment, cold, hunger, and general misery. One of his neighbors punched him in the ribs, asking roughly: "What's the matter with your cheek? In fine weather there's no holding you, youngster." Turning about with prudence he worked himself out of his coat and threw it over the boy. The other man closed up, muttering: "'Twill make a bloomin' man of you, sonny." They flung their arms over and pressed against him. Charley drew his feet up and his eyelids dropped. Sighs were heard, as men, perceiving that they were not to be "drowned in a hurry," tried easier positions. Mr. Creighton, who had hurt his leg, lay amongst us with compressed lips. Some fellows belonging to his watch set about securing him better. Without a word or a glance he lifted his arms one after another to facilitate the operation, and not a muscle moved in his stern, young face. They asked him with solicitude: "Easier now, sir?" He answered with a curt: "That'll do." He was a hard young officer, but many of his watch used to say they liked him well enough because he had "such a gentlemanly way of damning us up and down the deck." Others, unable to discern such fine shades of refinement, respected him for his smartness. For the first time since the ship had gone on her beam ends Captain Allistoun gave a short glance down at his men. He was almost upright—one foot against the side of the skylight, one knee on the deck; and with the end of the vang round his waist swung back and forth with his gaze fixed ahead, watchful, like a man looking out for a sign. Before his eyes the ship, with half her deck

below water, rose and fell on heavy seas that rushed from under her flashing in the cold sunshine. We began to think she was wonderfully buoyant—considering.

. . .

On the black sky the stars, coming out, gleamed over an inky sea that, speckled with foam, flashed back at them the evanescent and pale light of a dazzling whiteness born from the black turmoil of the waves. Remote in the eternal calm they glittered hard and cold above the uproar of the earth; they surrounded the vanquished and tormented ship on all sides: more pitiless than the eyes of a triumphant mob, and as unapproachable as the hearts of men.

The icy south wind howled exultingly under the somber splendor of the sky. The cold shook the men with a resistless violence as though it had tried to shake them to pieces. Short moans were swept unheard off the stiff lips. Some complained in mutters of "not feeling themselves below the waist"; while those who had closed their eyes, imagined they had a block of ice on their chests. Others, alarmed at not feeling any pain in their fingers, beat the deck feebly with their hands—obstinate and exhausted.

. . .

225

Knocked Down-III

"They've got some hot coffee. . . . Bosun got it. . . ." "No! . . . Where?" . . . "It's coming! Cook made it." . . .

The hot drink helped us through the bleak hours that precede the dawn. The sky low by the horizon took on the delicate tints of pink and yellow like the inside of a rare shell. And higher, where it glowed with a pearly sheen, a small black cloud appeared, like a forgotten fragment of the night set in a border of dazzling gold. The beams of light skipped on the crests of waves. The eyes of men turned to the eastward. The sunlight flooded their weary faces. They were giving themselves up to fatigue as though they had done forever with their work. On Singleton's black oilskin coat the dried salt glistened like hoar frost. He hung on by the wheel, with open and lifeless eyes. Captain Allistoun, unblinking, faced the rising sun. His lips stirred, opened for the first time in twenty-four hours, and with a fresh firm voice he cried, "Wear ship!"

The commanding sharp tones made all these torpid men start like a sudden flick of a whip. Then again, motionless where they lay, the force of habit made some of them repeat the order in hardly audible murmurs. Captain Allistoun glanced down at his crew, and several, with fumbling fingers and hopeless movements, tried to cast themselves adrift. He repeated impatiently, "Wear ship. Now then, Mr. Baker, get the men along. What's the matter with them?" "Wear ship. Do you hear there? Wear ship!" thundered out the boatswain suddenly. His voice seemed to break through a deadly spell. Men began to stir and crawl. "I want the fore topmast staysail run up smartly," said the master, very loudly; "if you can't manage it standing up you must do it lying down— that's all. Bear a hand!" "Come along! Let's give the old girl a chance," urged the boatswain. "Aye! aye! Wear ship!" exclaimed quavering voices. The forecastle men, with reluctant faces, prepared to go forward. Mr. Baker pushed ahead grunting on all fours to show the way, and they followed him over the break. The others lay still with a vile hope in their hearts of not being required to move till they got saved or drowned in peace.

After some time they could be seen forward appearing on the forecastle head, one by one in unsafe attitudes; hanging on to the rails; clambering over the anchors; embracing the crosshead of the windlass or hugging the forecapstan. They were restless with strange exertions, waved their arms, knelt, lay flat down, staggered up, seemed to strive their hardest to go overboard.

Suddenly a small white piece of canvas fluttered amongst them, grew larger, beating. Its narrow head rose in jerks—and at last it stood distended and triangular in the sunshine. "They have done it!" cried the voices aft. Captain Allistoun let go the rope he had round his wrist and rolled to leeward headlong. He could be seen casting the lee main braces off the pins while the backwash of waves splashed over him. "Square the main yard!" he shouted up to us—who stared at him in wonder. We hesitated to stir. "The main brace, men. Haul! haul anyhow! Lay on your backs and haul!" he screeched, half drowned down there. We did not believe we could move the main yard, but the strongest and the less discouraged tried to execute the order. Others assisted halfheartedly. Singleton's eyes blazed suddenly as he took a fresh grip of the spokes. Captain Allistoun fought his way up to windward. "Haul, men! Try to move it! Haul, and help the ship." His hard face worked suffused and furious. "Is she going off, Singleton?" he cried. "Not a move yet, sir," croaked the old seaman in a horribly hoarse voice. "Watch the helm, Singleton," spluttered the master. "Haul, men! Have you no more strength than rats? Haul, and earn your salt." Mr. Creighton, on his back, with a swollen leg and a face as white as a piece of paper, blinked his eyes; his bluish lips twitched. In the wild scramble men grabbed at him, crawled over his hurt leg, knelt on his chest. He kept perfectly still, setting his teeth without a moan, without a sigh. The master's ardor, the cries of that silent man inspired us. We hauled and hung in bunches on the rope. We heard him say with violence to Donkin, who sprawled abjectly on his stomach, "I will brain you with this belaying pin if you don't catch hold of the brace," and that victim of men's injustice, cowardly and cheeky, whimpered: "Are you goin' ter murder hus now," while with sudden desperation he gripped the rope. Men sighed, shouted, hissed meaningless words, groaned. The yards moved, came slowly square against the wind, that hummed loudly on the yardarms. "Going off, sir," shouted Singleton, "she's just started." "Catch a turn with that brace. Catch a turn!" clamored the master. Mr. Creighton, nearly suffocated and unable to move, made a mighty effort, and with his left hand managed to nip the rope. "All fast!" cried someone. He closed his eyes as if going off into a swoon, while huddled together about the brace we watched with scared looks what the ship would do now.

Knocked Down–IV

She went off slowly as though she had been weary and disheartened like the men she carried. She paid off very gradually, making us hold our breath till we choked, and as soon as she had brought the wind abaft the beam she started to move, and fluttered our hearts. It was awful to see her, nearly overturned, begin to gather way and drag her submerged side through the water. The deadeyes of the rigging churned the breaking seas. The lower half of the deck was full of mad whirlpools and eddies; and the long line of the lee rail could be seen showing black now and then in the swirls of a field of foam as dazzling and white as a field of snow. The wind sang shrilly amongst the spars; and at every slight lurch we expected her to slip to the bottom sideways from under our backs. When dead before it she made the first distinct attempt to stand up, and we encouraged her with a feeble and discordant howl. A great sea came running up aft and hung for a moment over us with a curling top; then crashed down under the counter and spread out on both sides into a great sheet of bursting froth. Above its fierce hiss we heard Singleton's croak: "She is steering!" He had both his feet now planted firmly on the grating, and the wheel spun fast as he eased the helm. "Bring the wind on the port quarter and steady her!" called out the master, staggering to his feet, the first man up from amongst our prostrate heap. One or two screamed with excitement: "She rises!" Far away forward, Mr. Baker and three others were seen erect and black on the clear sky, lifting their arms, and with open mouths as though they had been shouting all together. The ship trembled, trying to lift her side, lurched back, seemed to give up with a nerveless dip, and suddenly with an unexpected jerk swung violently to windward, as though she had torn herself out from a deadly grasp. The whole immense volume of water, lifted by her deck, was thrown bodily across to starboard.

Loud cracks were heard. Iron ports breaking open thundered with ringing blows. The water topped over the starboard rail with the rush of a river falling over a dam. The sea on deck, and the seas on every side of her, mingled together in a deafening roar. She rolled violently. We got up and were helplessly run or flung about from side to side. Men, rolling over and over, yelled, "The house will go!" "She clears herself!" Lifted by a towering sea she ran along with it for a moment, spouting thick streams of water through every opening of her wounded sides. The lee braces having been carried away or washed off the pins, all the ponderous yards on the fore swung from side to side and with appalling rapidity at every roll. The men forward were seen crouching here and there with fearful glances upwards at the enormous spars that whirled about over their heads. The torn canvas and the ends of broken gear streamed in the wind like wisps of hair. Through the clear sunshine, over the flashing turmoil and uproar of the seas, the ship ran blindly, disheveled and headlong, as if fleeing for her life; and on the poop we spun, we tottered about, distracted and noisy. We all spoke at once in a thin babble; we had the aspect of invalids and the gestures of maniacs. Eyes shone, large and haggard, in smiling, meager faces that seemed to have been dusted over with powdered chalk. We stamped, clapped our hands, feeling ready to jump and do anything, but in reality hardly able to keep on our feet. Captain Allistoun, hard and slim, gesticulated madly from the poop at Mr. Baker: "Steady these foreyards! Steady them the best you can!" On the main deck, men excited by his cries, splashed, dashing aimlessly here and there with the foam swirling up to their waists. Apart, far aft, and alone by the helm, old Singleton had deliberately tucked his white beard under the top button of his glistening coat. Swaying upon the din and tumult of the seas, with the whole battered length of the ship launched forward in a rolling rush before his steady old eyes, he stood rigidly still, forgotten by all, and with an attentive face. In front of his erect figure only the two arms moved crosswise with a swift and sudden readiness, to check or urge again the rapid stir of circling spokes. He steered with care.

· · ·

The master and Mr. Baker coming face to face stared for a moment, with the intense and amazed looks of men meeting unexpectedly after years of trouble. Their voices were gone, and they whispered desperately at one another. "Anyone missing?" asked Captain Allistoun. "No. All there." "Anybody hurt?" "Only the second mate." "I will look after him directly. We're lucky." "Very," articulated Mr. Baker, faintly. He gripped the rail and rolled bloodshot eyes. The little gray man made an effort to raise his voice above a dull mutter, and fixed his chief mate with a cold gaze, piercing like a dart. "Get sail on the ship," he said, speaking authoritatively, and with an inflexible snap of his thin lips. "Get sail on her as soon as you can. This is a fair wind. At once, sir—don't give the men time to feel themselves. They will get done up and stiff, and we will never . . . We must get her along now." . . . He reeled to a long heavy roll; the rail dipped into the glancing hissing water. He caught a shroud, swung helplessly against the mate . . . "now we have a fair wind at last. Make—sail." His head rolled from shoulder to shoulder. His eyelids began to beat rapidly. "And the pumps—pumps, Mr. Baker."

· · ·

Knocked Down-v

The pump rods, clanking, stamped in short jumps while the flywheels turned smoothly, with great speed, at the foot of the mainmast, flinging back and forth with a regular impetuosity two limp clusters of men clinging to the handles. They abandoned themselves, swaying from the hip with twitching faces and stony eyes. The carpenter, sounding from time to time, exclaimed mechanically: "Shake her up! Keep her going!" Mr. Baker could not speak, but found his voice to shout; and under the goad of his objurgations, men looked to the lashings, dragged out new sails; and thinking themselves unable to move, carried heavy blocks aloft—overhauled the gear. They went up the rigging with faltering and desperate efforts. Their heads swam as they shifted their hold, stepped blindly on the yards like men in the dark; or trusted themselves to the first rope to hand with the negligence of exhausted strength. The narrow escapes from falls did not disturb the languid beat of their hearts; the roar of the seas seething far below them sounded continuous and faint like an indistinct noise from another world: the wind filled their eyes with tears, and with heavy gusts tried to push them off from where they swayed in insecure positions. With streaming faces and blowing hair they flew up and down between sky and water, bestriding the ends of yardarms, crouching on foot ropes, embracing lifts to have their hands free, or standing up against chain ties. Their thoughts floated vaguely between the desire of rest and the desire of life, while their stiffened fingers cast off head-earrings, fumbled for knives, or held with tenacious grip against the violent shocks of beating canvas. They glared savagely at one another, made frantic signs with one hand while they held their life in the other, looked down on the narrow strip of flooded deck, shouted along to leeward: "Light-to!" . . . "Haul out!" . . . "Make fast!" Their lips moved, their eyes started, furious and eager with the desire to be understood, but the wind tossed their words unheard upon the disturbed sea. In an unendurable and unending strain they worked like men driven by a merciless dream to toil in an atmosphere of ice or flame. They burnt and shivered in turns. Their eyeballs smarted as if in the smoke of a conflagration; their heads were ready to burst with every shout. Hard fingers seemed to grip their throats. At every roll they thought: Now I must let go. It will shake us all off—and thrown about aloft they cried wildly: "Look out there—catch the end." "Reeve clear." . . . "Turn this block. . . ." They nodded desperately; shook infuriated faces, "No! No! From down up." They seemed to hate one another with a deadly hate. The longing to be done with it all gnawed their breasts, and the wish to do things well was a burning pain.

· · ·

Stowing the Mainsail

A.Briscoe/30

Knocked Down–VI

Mr. Baker, feeling very weak, tottered here and there, grunting and inflexible, like a man of iron. He waylaid those who, coming from aloft, stood gasping for breath. He ordered, encouraged, scolded. "Now then—to the main-topsail now! Tally on to that gantline. Don't stand about there!" "Is there no rest for us?" muttered voices. He spun round fiercely, with a sinking heart. "No! No rest till the work is done. Work till you drop. That's what you're here for." A bowed seaman at his elbow gave a short laugh. "Do or die," he croaked bitterly, then spat into his broad palms, swung up his long arms, and grasping the rope high above his head sent out a mournful, wailing cry for a pull all together. A sea boarded the quarter-deck and sent the whole lot sprawling to leeward. Caps, handspikes floated. Clenched hands, kicking legs, with here and there a spluttering face, stuck out of the white hiss of foaming water. Mr. Baker, knocked down with the rest, screamed, "Don't let go that rope! Hold on to it! Hold!" And sorely bruised by the brutal fling, they held on to it, as though it had been the fortune of their life. The ship ran, rolling heavily, and the topping crests glanced past port and starboard flashing their white heads. Pumps were freed. Braces were rove. The three topsails and foresail were set. She spurted faster over the water, outpacing the swift rush of waves. The menacing thunder of distanced seas rose behind her—filled the air with the tremendous vibrations of its voice. And devastated, battered, and wounded she drove foaming to the northward, as though inspired by the courage of a high endeavor. . . .

A Halyard Chantey

All hands were called to make sail, and as we manned the main tops'l halyards Jimmy Marshall jumped to the pin rail, and with one leg over the top of the bulwark, he faced the line of men tailing along the deck.

"A chantey, boys!" shouted Mr. Stoddard as he took his place "beforehand" on the rope. "Come now, run her up, lads. *Up! Up!*" and the heavy yard commenced to creep along the mast to the sound of the creaking parral, the complaining of the blocks, and the haunting deep sea tune of "Blow the Man Down," greatest of all the two haul chanteys.

JIMMY—"*Now rouse her right up boys for Liverpool town,*"
SAILORS—"*Go way—way—blow the man down.*"
JIMMY—"*We'll blow the man up and blow the man down,*"
SAILORS—"*Oh, give us some time to blow the man down.*"
JIMMY—"*We lay off the Island of Maderdegascar.*"
SAILORS—"*Hi! Ho! Blow the man down.*"
JIMMY—"*We lowered three anchors to make her hold faster,*"
SAILORS—"*Oh, give us some time to blow the man down.*"

CHORUS

All hands—"*Then we'll blow the man up,*
    And we'll blow the man down,
    Go way—way—blow the man down.
    We'll blow him right over to Liverpool town,
    Oh, give us some time to blow the man down.
    Ho! Stand by your braces,
    And stand by your falls;
    Hi! Ho! Blow the man down,
    We'll blow him clean over to Liverpool town,
    Oh, give us some time to blow the man down."

Old Marshall faced to windward, his mustache lifting in the breeze, the grey weather worn fringe of hair bending up over his battered nose. He always sang with a full quid in his cheek, and the absence of several front teeth helped to give a peculiar deep-sea quality to his voice.

What the Old Man Said

"Don't you take no sail off 'er,"
    The Ol' Man said,
Wind an' sea rampagin'
    Fit to wake the dead.

Thrashin' through the Forties
    In the sleet and 'ail,
Runnin' down the Eastin'
    Under all plain sail.

"She's loggin' seventeen
    An' she's liftin' to it grand,
So I'm goin' below
    For a stretch off the land.

"An' if it gits any worse, Mister,
    You can come an' call me,
But—don't you take no sail off 'er,"
Said the Ol' Man—
    Said 'e!

Them was the days, sonnies,
    Them was the men,
Them was the ships
    As we'll never see again.

Oh, but it was somethin'
    Then to be alive—
Thrashin' under royals
    South o' Forty-five . . .

When it was—"Don't you take no sail off 'er,"
    The Ol' Man'd say,
Beard an' whiskers starin'
    Stiff with frozen spray—

"She's loggin' seventeen
    An' she's liftin' to it grand,
An' I mean to keep 'er goin'
    Under all she'll stand.

"An' if it gits any worse, Mister,
    You can send an' call me,
But—don't you take no sail off 'er,"
Said the Ol' Man—
    Said 'e!

Crack It On

Aye! We're heading back for home men,
Drive the ship through wrack and foam then,
        Crack it on! Crack it on!
With a steady hand a-helming,
Trampling down the seas o'er whelming,
        Crack it on you bullies! Crack it on!
For there's someone home to meet you,
Maybe mothers old to greet you,
There are anxious wives a-waiting, when port is won,
There'll be land-lights winking, beaming,
There'll be gold coins clinking, gleaming,
        So crack it on you bullies! Crack it on!!

For our craft is swift and cunning,
Wise she is to where we're running,
        Crack it on! Crack it on!
Watch the spindrift breaking, drifting,
"Keep those weather leeches lifting!"
        Crack it on you bullies, crack it on!!
There'll be those to hear worth hearing,
There'll be clothes to wear worth wearing,
For we're weary, homeward bounders, every mother's son,
There'll be things worth going after—
Food and song and lights and laughter,
        So crack it on you bullies! Crack it on!!

What of lightning's fingers livid,
Teeth of storm dogs, bared and vivid,
              Crack it on! Crack it on!
Though the skies should split asunder,
With the dooming drums of thunder,
              Crack it on you bullies, crack it on!!
Though the gales should lash and harry,
Pile on all the rags she'll carry,
Listen to the reef-points drum, and tautened back-stays drone;
Up and down the "Old Man" paces,
"Keep the padlocks on those braces!" —
              So keep them on you bullies—keep them on!

Though the gales should rip and tear you,
And the toil and moil should wear you,
              Crack it on! Crack it on!
Though you're less than any slave is,
And you're ready for old Davey's,
              Crack it on you bullies, crack it on!!
'Spite of Hell or heavy weather,
Heave her!—bust her!—all together!
And we'll show the Lapland Sorceress how things are done,
Leap and jump and dash for cover,
When she sends those green ones over,
              So crack it on you bullies! Crack it on!!

Haul and strain and sweat my hearties,
Sailing back to where your heart is,
              Crack it on! Crack it on!
Though you're famined, fagged and windtost,
Devil plague and take the hindmost,
              Crack it on you bullies, crack it on!!
For there's gin-mills filled with liquor,
Dames with eyes that smile and flicker
And who'll swear to God above, she loves but you alone,
Aye! She'll love and rob you, brother,
Then heave you out to love another,
              So crack it on you bullies! Crack it on!!

Sons of sin and sons of no hope,
Homeland ladies have the tow-rope,
              Crack it on! Crack it on!
Through with ocean's wet and watches
Far from sea-boils, cuts, and blotches,
              Crack it on you bullies, crack it on!!
Can't you see old Ratcliffe Highway,
Fav'rite haunt and pleasant by-way,
Oh for a dry and cosy bed to lie and laze upon,
Far from tough Mate's crazy notions,
Far from things that are the ocean's,
              So crack it on you bullies! Crack it on!!

Dipping flags to laden far sails,
Deep with horns, bones, hides and parcels,
              Crack it on! Crack it on!
We will be back home before you,
And we'll tell them where we saw you;
              Crack it on you bullies, crack it on!!
Willing hands to wear and steer her,
Getting near and ever nearer,
We'll beat against the breath of bold Euroclydon;
Up through Channel quickly homing,
They will telegraph our coming,
              So crack it on you bullies! Crack it on!!

We'll be done with ships—we'll show them,
When we furl those sails and stow them,
              Crack it on! Crack it on!!
We'll forget the Cape Horn fever,
Singing, "Leave her Johnny leave her,"
              Crack it on you bullies, crack it on!!
But 'twill be the same old story,
With our pay all shot to glory;
We'll be in the hands of "runners," before we're done,
Drunk or starved, and past all caring,
Come down broke for more sea-faring.
              So crack it on, and keep on, cracking on!

Eight Bells

Four double strokes repeated on the bells,
And then away, away the shufflers go
Aft to the darkness where the ruler dwells,
Where by the rail he sucks his pipe aglow;
Beside him his relief looks down on those below.

There in the dark they answer to their names,
Those dozen men, and one relieves the wheel,
One the look-out, the others sit to games
In moonlight, backed against the bulkhead's steel,
In the lit patch the hands flick, card by card, the deal.

Meanwhile the men relieved are forward all,
Some in their bunks asleep, while others sing
Low-voiced some ditty of the halliard-fall,
The ship impels them on with stooping wing,
Rolling and roaring on with triumph in her swing.

Killing Time

I commenced a deliberate system of time-killing, which united some profit with a cheering up of the heavy hours. As soon as I came on deck, and took my place and regular walk, I began with repeating over to myself a string of matters which I had in my memory, in regular order. First, the multiplication table and the tables of weights and measures; then the states of the union, with their capitals; the counties of England, with their shire towns; the kings of England in their order; and a large part of the peerage, which I committed from an almanac that we had on board; and then the Kanaka numerals. This carried me through my facts, and, being repeated deliberately, with long intervals, often eked out the two first bells. Then came the ten commandments; the thirty-ninth chapter of Job, and a few other passages from Scripture. The next in the order, that I never varied from, came Cowper's Casta-way, which was a great favorite with me; the solemn measure and gloomy character of which, as well as the incident that it was founded upon, made it well suited to a lonely watch at sea. Then his lines to Mary, his address to the jackdaw, and a short extract from Table Talk; (I abounded in Cowper, for I happened to have a volume of his poems in my chest;) "Ille et nefasto" from Horace, and Gœthe's Erl King. After I had got through these, I allowed myself a more general range among everything that I could re-member, both in prose and verse. In this way, with an occasional break by relieving the wheel, heaving the log, and going to the scuttle-butt for a drink of water, the longest watch was passed away; and I was so regular in my silent recitations, that if there was no interruption by ship's duty, I could tell very nearly the number of bells by my progress.

Scrub Down

Soon after eight o'clock, the appearance of the ship gave evidence that this was the first Sunday we had yet had in fine weather. As the sun came up clear, with the promise of a fair, warm day, and, as usual on Sunday, there was no work going on, all hands turned-to upon clearing out the forecastle. The wet and soiled clothes which had accumulated there during the past month, were brought up on deck; the chests moved; brooms, buckets of water, swabs, scrubbing-brushes, and scrapers carried down, and applied, until the forecastle floor was as white as chalk, and everything neat and in order. The bedding from the berths was then spread on deck, and dried and aired; the deck-tub filled with water, and a grand washing begun on all the clothes which were brought up. Shirts, frocks, drawers, trousers, jackets, stockings, of every shape and color, wet and dirty—many of them moldy from having been lying a long time wet in a foul corner—these were all washed and scrubbed out, and finally towed overboard for half an hour; and then made fast in the rigging to dry. Wet boots and shoes were spread out to dry in sunny places on decks; and the whole ship looked like a back yard on a washing day. After we had done with our clothes, we began upon our own persons. A little fresh water, which we had saved from our allowance, was put in buckets, and, with soap and towels, we had what sailors call a fresh-water wash.

The same bucket, to be sure, had to go through several hands, and was spoken for by one after another, but as we rinsed off in salt water, pure from the ocean, and the fresh was used only to start the accumulated grime and blackness of five weeks, it was held of little consequence. We soaped down and scrubbed one another with towels and pieces of canvas, stripping to it; and then, getting into the head, threw buckets of water upon each other. After this, came shaving, and combing, and brushing; and when, having spent the first part of the day in this way, we sat down on the forecastle, in the afternoon, with clean duck trousers, and shirts on, washed, and shaved and combed, and looking a dozen shades lighter for it, reading, sewing and talking at our ease, with a clear sky and warm sun over our heads, a steady breeze over the larboard quarter, studding-sails out alow and aloft, and all the flying kites abroad—we felt that we had got back into the pleasantest part of a sailor's life. At sun-down the clothes were all taken down from the rigging—clean and dry—and stowed neatly away in our chests; and our south-westers, thick boots, guernsey frocks, and other accompaniments of bad weather, put out of the way, we hoped for the rest of the voyage, as we expected to come upon the coast early in the autumn.

Moonlight

One night, while we were in these tropics, I went out to the end of
the flying-jib-boom, upon some duty, and, having finished it,
turned round, and lay over the boom for a long time, admiring the
beauty of the sight before me. Being so far from the deck, I could
look at the ship, as at a separate vessel;—and, there rose up from
the water, supported only by the small black hull, a pyramid of
canvas, spreading out far beyond the hull, and towering up almost,
as it seemed in the indistinct night air, to the clouds. The sea was as
still as an inland lake; the light trade-wind was gently and steadily
breathing from astern; the dark blue sky was studded with the
tropical stars; there was no sound but the rippling of the water
under the stem; and the sails were spread out, wide and high;—
the two lower studding-sails stretching, on each side, far beyond
the deck; the top-mast studding-sails, like wings to the topsails;
the top-gallant studding-sails spreading fearlessly out above them;
still higher, the two royal studding-sails, looking like two kites
flying from the same string; and, highest of all, the little skysail,
the apex of the pyramid, seeming actually to touch the stars, and to
be out of reach of human hand. So quiet, too, was the sea, and so
steady the breeze, that if these sails had been sculptured marble,
they could not have been more motionless. Not a ripple upon the
surface of the canvas; not even a quivering of the extreme edges of
the sail—so perfectly were they distended by the breeze. I was so
lost in the sight, that I forgot the presence of the man who came out
with me, until he said (for he, too, rough old man-of-war's-man as
he was, had been gazing at the show), half to himself, still looking
at the marble sails—"How quietly they do their work!"

Getting Ready

All the first part of a passage is spent in getting a ship ready for sea, and the last part in getting her ready for port. She is, as sailors say, like a lady's watch, always out of repair. The new, strong sails, which we had up off Cape Horn, were to be sent down, and the old set, which were still serviceable in fine weather, to be bent in their place; all the rigging to be set up, fore and aft; the masts stayed; the standing rigging to be tarred down; lower and top-mast rigging rattled down, fore and aft; the ship scraped, inside and out, and painted; decks varnished; new and neat knots, seizings and coverings to be fitted; and every part put in order, to look well to the owner's eye, on coming into Boston. This, of course, was a long matter; and all hands were kept on deck at work for the whole of each day, during the rest of the voyage. Sailors call this hard usage; but the ship must be in crack order, and "we're homeward bound" was the answer to everything.

The Landfall-1

A week afterwards the *Narcissus* entered the chops of the Channel.

Under white wings she skimmed low over the blue sea like a great tired bird speeding to its nest. The clouds raced with her mastheads; they rose astern enormous and white, soared to the zenith, flew past, and falling down the wide curve of the sky seemed to dash headlong into the sea—the clouds swifter than the ship, more free, but without a home. The coast to welcome her stepped out of space into the sunshine. The lofty headlands trod masterfully into the sea; the wide bays smiled in the light; the shadows of homeless clouds ran along the sunny plains, leaped over valleys, without a check darted up the hills, rolled down the slopes; and the sunshine pursued them with patches of running brightness. On the brows of dark cliffs white lighthouses shone in pillars of light. The Channel glittered like a blue mantle shot with gold and starred by the silver of the capping seas. The *Narcissus* rushed past the headlands and the bays. Outward-bound vessels crossed her track, lying over, and with their masts stripped for a slogging fight with the hard sou'-wester. And, inshore, a string of smoking steamboats waddled, hugging the coast, like migrating and amphibious monsters, distrustful of the restless waves.

The Landfall–II

At night the headlands retreated, the bays advanced into one unbroken line of gloom. The lights of the earth mingled with the lights of heaven; and above the tossing lanterns of a trawling fleet a great lighthouse shone steadily, such as an enormous riding light burning above a vessel of fabulous dimensions. Below its steady glow, the coast, stretching away straight and black, resembled the high side of an indestructible craft riding motionless upon the immortal and unresting sea. The dark land lay alone in the midst of waters, like a mighty ship bestarred with vigilant lights—a ship carrying the burden of millions of lives—a ship freighted with dross and with jewels, with gold and with steel. She towered up immense and strong, guarding priceless traditions and untold suffering, sheltering glorious memories and base forgetfulness, ignoble virtues and splendid transgressions. A great ship! For ages had the ocean battered in vain her enduring sides; she was there when the world was vaster and darker, when the sea was great and mysterious, and ready to surrender the prize of fame to audacious men. A ship mother of fleets and nations! The great flagship of the race; stronger than the storms, and anchored in the open sea.

The Bell Buoy Speaks

They christened my brother of old—
  And a saintly name he bears—
They gave him his place to hold
  At the head of the belfry-stairs,
  Where the minster-towers stand
And the breeding kestrels cry.
  Would I change with my brother a league inland?
(Shoal! 'Ware shoal!) Not I!

In the flush of the hot June prime,
  O'er smooth flood-tides afire,
I hear him hurry the chime
  To the bidding of checked Desire;
  Till the sweated ringers tire
And the wild bob-majors die.
  Could I wait for my turn in the godly choir?
(Shoal! 'Ware shoal!) Not I!

When the smoking scud is blown,
  When the greasy wind-rack lowers,
Apart and at peace and alone,
  He counts the changeless hours.
  He wars with darkling Powers
(I war with a darkling sea);
  Would he stoop to my work in the gusty mirk?
(Shoal! 'Ware shoal!) Not he!

There was never a priest to pray,
  There was never a hand to toll,
When they made me guard of the bay,
  And moored me over the shoal.
  I rock, I reel, and I roll—
My four great hammers ply—
  Could I speak or be still at the Church's will?
(Shoal! 'Ware shoal!) Not I!

The landward marks have failed,
  The fog-bank glides unguessed,
The seaward lights are veiled,
  The spent deep feigns her rest:
  But my ear is laid to her breast,

I lift to the swell—I cry!
  Could I wait in sloth on the Church's oath?
(Shoal! 'Ware shoal!) Not I!

At the careless end of night
  I thrill to the nearing screw;
I turn in the clearing light
  And I call to the drowsy crew;
  And the mud boils foul and blue
As the blind bow backs away.
  Will they give me their thanks if they clear the banks?
(Shoal! 'Ware shoal!) Not they!

The beach-pools cake and skim,
  The bursting spray-heads freeze,
I gather on crown and rim
  The grey, grained ice of the seas,
  Where, sheathed from bitt to trees,
The plunging colliers lie.
  Would I barter my place for the Church's grace?
(Shoal! 'Ware shoal!) Not I!

Through the blur of the whirling snow,
  Or the black of the inky sleet,
The lanterns gather and grow,
  And I look for the homeward fleet.
  Rattle of block and sheet—
"Ready about—stand by!"
  Shall I ask them a fee ere they fetch the quay?
(Shoal! 'Ware shoal!) Not I!

I dip and I surge and I swing
  In the rip of the racing tide,
By the gates of doom I sing,
  On the horns of death I ride.
  A ship-length overside,
Between the course and the sand,
  Fretted and bound I bide
    Peril whereof I cry.
  Would I change with my brother a league inland?
(Shoal! 'Ware shoal!) Not I!

The Homecoming–1

A summer day with a sea turn in the wind. The Grand Banks fog, rolling in wave after wave, is dissolved by the perfumed breath of New England hayfields into a gentle haze that turns the State House dome to old gold, films brick walls with a soft patina, and sifts blue shadows among the foliage of the Common elms. Out of the mist in Massachusetts Bay comes riding a clipper ship, with the effortless speed of an albatross. Her proud commander keeps skysails and studdingsails set past Boston Light. After the long voyage she is in the pink of condition. Paintwork is spotless, decks holystoned cream-white, shrouds freshly tarred, ratlines square. Viewed through a powerful glass, her seizings, flemish-eyes, splices, and pointings are the perfection of the old-time art of rigging. The chafing-gear has just been removed, leaving spars and shrouds immaculate. The boys touched up her skysail poles with white paint, as she crossed the bay. Boom-ending her studdingsails and hauling a few points on the wind to shoot the Narrows, between Georges and Gallups and Lovells islands, she pays off again through President Road, and comes booming up the stream, a sight so beautiful that even the lounging soldiers at the Castle, persistent baiters of passing crews, are dumb with wonder and admiration.

The Homecoming-II

Colored pennants on Telegraph Hill have announced her coming to all who know the code. Topliff's News Room breaks into a buzz of conversation, comparing records and guessing at freight money; owners and agents walk briskly down State Street; counting-room clerks hang out of windows to watch her strike skysails and royals; the crimps and hussies of Ann Street foregather, to offer Jack a few days' scabrous pleasure before selling him to a new master. By the time the ship has reached the inner harbor, thousands of critical eyes are watching her every movement, quick to note if in any respect the mate has failed to make sailormen out of her crew of broken Argonauts, beachcombers, Kanakas, and Lascars.

The "old man" stalks the quarterdeck in top hat and frock coat, with the proper air of detachment; but the first mate is as busy as the devil in a gale of wind. Off India Wharf the ship rounds into the wind with a graceful curve, crew leaping into the rigging to furl topgallant sails as if shot upward by the blast of profanity from the mate's bull-like throat. With backed topsails her way is checked, and the cable rattles out of the chain lockers for the first time since Shanghai. Sails are clewed up. Yards are braced to a perfect parallel, and running-gear neatly coiled down.

The Homecoming–III

A warp is passed from capstan to stringer, and all hands on the
capstan bars walk her up to the wharf with the closing chantey of
a deep-sea voyage:

Solo

I. O, the times are hard and the wa - ges low,

Chorus;   Solo

Leave her, John - ny, leave her;   I'll pack my bag and

Chorus

go be - low;   It's time for us to leave her.

Farewell

They had secured their beauty to the dock,
First having decked her to delight the eye.
After long months of water and sky
These twenty saw the prison doors unlock;

These twenty men were free to quit the ship,
To tread dry land and slumber when they chose,
To count no bells that counted their repose,
To waken free from python Duty's grip.

What they had suffered and had greatly been
Was stamped upon their faces; they were still
Haggard with the indomitable will
That singleness of purpose had made clean.

These twenty threadbare men with frost-bit ears
And canvas bags and little chests of gears.

Servant-Queen

You swept across the waters like a Queen,
Finding a path where never trackway showed,
Daylong you coultered the ungarnered clean
Casting your travelling shadow as you strode.

And in the nights, when lamps were lit, you sped
With gleams running beside you, like to hounds,
Swift, swift, a dappled glitter of light shed
On snatching sprays above collapsing mounds.

And after many a calm and many a storm,
Nearing the land, your sailors saw arise
The pinnacles of snow where streamers form,
And the ever-dying surf that never dies.

Then, laden with Earth's spoils, you used to come
Back, from the ocean's beauty to the roar
Of all the hammers of the mills of home,
Your wandering sailors dragged you to the shore,

Singing, to leave you muted and inert,
A moping place for sea-gulls in the rain
While city strangers trod you with their dirt,
And landsmen loaded you for sea again.

WILLIAM H. DRURY / RUDYARD KIPLING

His Sea

Who hath desired the Sea? —the sight of salt water unbounded —
The heave and the halt and the hurl and the crash of the comber wind-hounded?
The sleek-barrelled swell before storm, grey, foamless, enormous, and growing —
Stark calm on the lap of the Line or the crazy-eyed hurricane blowing —
His Sea in no showing the same —his Sea and the same 'neath each showing:
   His Sea as she slackens or thrills?
So and no otherwise —so and no otherwise —hillmen desire their Hills!

Who hath desired the Sea? —the immense and contemptuous surges?
The shudder, the stumble, the swerve, as the star-stabbing bowsprit emerges?
The orderly clouds of the Trades, the ridged, roaring sapphire thereunder —
Unheralded cliff-haunting flaws and the headsail's low-volleying thunder —
His Sea in no wonder the same —his Sea and the same through each wonder:
   His Sea as she rages or stills?
So and no otherwise —so and no otherwise —hillmen desire their Hills.

Who hath desired the Sea? Her menaces swift as her mercies?
The in-rolling walls of the fog and the silver-winged breeze that disperses?
The unstable mined berg going South and the calvings and groans that declare it —
White water half-guessed overside and the moon breaking timely to bare it;
His Sea as his fathers have dared —his Sea as his children shall dare it:
   His Sea as she serves him or kills?
So and no otherwise —so and no otherwise —hillmen desire their Hills.

Who hath desired the Sea? Her excellent loneliness rather
Than forecourts of kings, and her outermost pits than the streets where men gather
Inland, among dust, under trees —inland where the slayer may slay him —
Inland, out of reach of her arms, and the bosom whereon he must lay him —
His Sea from the first that betrayed —at the last that shall never betray him:
   His Sea that his being fulfils?
So and no otherwise —so and no otherwise —hillmen desire their Hills.

Sailor's Return

The gray sea and the long black land;
And the yellow half-moon large and low;
And the startled little waves that leap
In fiery ringlets from their sleep,
As I gain the cove with pushing prow,
And quench its speed in the slushy sand.

Then a mile of warm sea-scented beach;
Three fields to cross till a farm appears;
A tap at the pane, the quick sharp scratch
And blue spurt of a lighted match,
And a voice less loud, through its joys and fears,
Than the two hearts beating each to each!

269

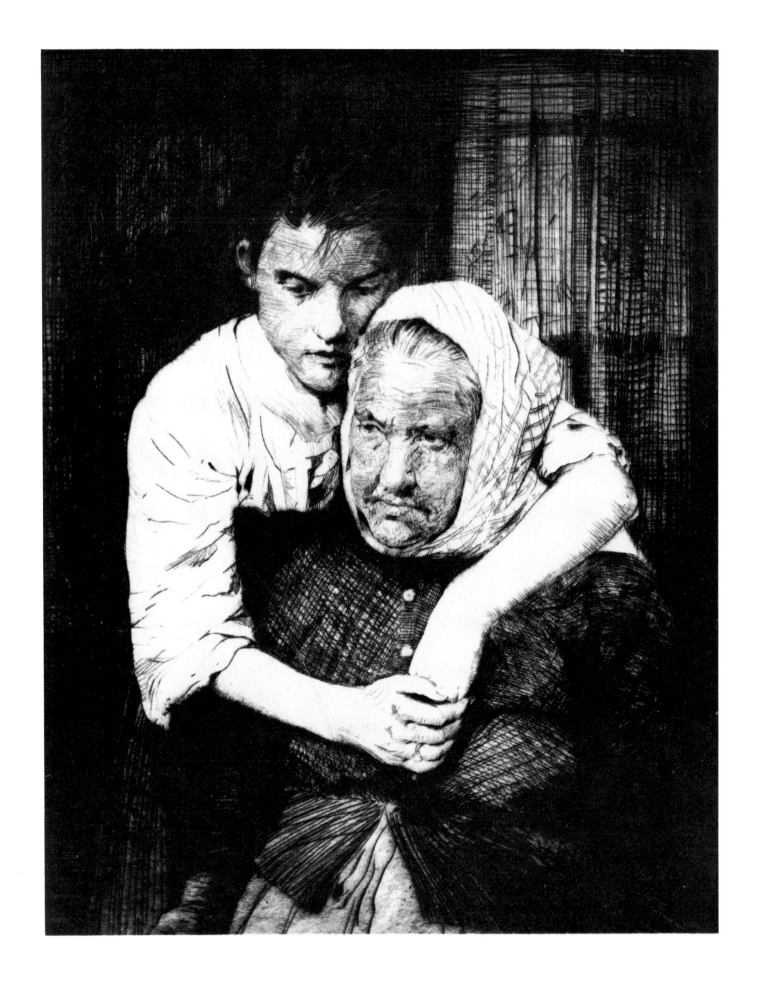

Posted as Missing

"Have you news of my boy Jack?"
>*Not this tide.*
"When d'you think that he'll come back?"
>*Not with this wind blowing, and this tide.*

"Has any one else had word of him?"
>*Not this tide.*
For what is sunk will hardly swim,
>*Not with this wind blowing, and this tide.*

"Oh, dear, what comfort can I find?"
>*None this tide,*
>*Nor any tide,*
Except he did not shame his kind—
>*Not even with the wind blowing, and that tide.*

Then hold your head up all the more,
>*This tide,*
>*And every tide;*
Because he was the son you bore,
>*And gave to that wind blowing and that tide!*

WILLIAM LEE-HANKEY / RUDYARD KIPLING   271

Who Pilots Ships

Who pilots ships knows all a heart can know
Of beauty, and his eyes may close in death
And be content. There is no wind to blow
Whiter than foam-white and no wind's breath
Sweeter than tropic wind. There is no star
That throbs with cold white fire as North stars do,
No golden moon-path lovelier than the far
Path burning on the sea when dusk is blue.
There is no rain so swift as rain that flies
In bright battalions with a storm begun,
No song that shakes the heart like amber cries
Of gulls with wings turned yellow in the sun.
Who pilots ships, when life's last heart beat stop,
Has drained the cup of beauty drop by drop.

They Built Great Ships and Sailed Them

These splendid ships, each with her grace, her glory,
Her memory of old song or comrade's story,
Still in my mind the image of life's need,
Beauty in hardest action, beauty indeed.
"They built great ships and sailed them" sounds most brave
Whatever arts we have or fail to have;
I touch my country's mind, I come to grips
With half her purpose, thinking of these ships
That art untouched by softness, all that line
Drawn ringing hard to stand the test of brine,
That nobleness and grandeur, all that beauty
Born of a manly life and bitter duty,
That splendour of fine bows which yet could stand
The shock of rollers never checked by land.
That art of masts, sail crowded, fit to break,
Yet stayed to strength and backstayed into rake,
The life demanded by that art, the keen
Eye-puckered, hard-case seamen, silent, lean,—
They are grander things than all the art of towns,
Their tests are tempests and the sea that drowns,
They are my country's line, her great art done
By strong brains labouring on the thought unwon,
They mark our passage as a race of men,
Earth will not see such ships as those again.

The Old Breed

They cheered her from the waterside,
　　They watched her from the shore
Drop swiftly down the Mersey tide
　　Till she was seen no more,
Till, stately-swaying, tall and proud,
　　Her tower of sail grew dim,
And faded like a summer cloud
　　Beyond the far sea-rim.

They passed—like summer clouds they passed,
　　As fleeting and as fair:
The shapely hull, the soaring mast,
　　The speed beyond compare:
The hemp, the teak, the brasses bright,
　　The sunlit sails ashine,
The paint, the planking scoured and white,
　　The spars of glistening pine.

They passed—the ships, the men likewise,
　　The captains tried and bold,
The rich in lore of seas and skies,
　　The mates of mighty mould,
The bawling bosuns heard afar,
　　Sea craftsmen, Chips and Sails,
The crews whose veins ran Stockholm tar,
　　Big-fisted, hard as nails.

Long turned their log-book's final page!
　　Far South'ard now no more
Their royals dare the Forties' rage
　　As they were wont of yore.
No more, no more from Salthouse Dock
　　For lands of gold they clear,
Or, homebound, welcome off the Rock
　　The tugboat with a cheer.

What then remains? . . . The gulls, the breeze,
　　They bear from near and far
No word of Empress of the Seas,
　　Red Jacket, Shalimar,
But long as call the Mersey gulls
　　And Mersey tides do run,
The breed that drove the clipper hulls
　　Lives on from sire to son.

Clipper and liner, steam and sail,
　　The old law guides them still,
The ancient, stark sea needs prevail
　　Of courage, foresight, skill,
As when they ran the easting down
　　(Oh blow, my bully boys, blow!)
In clipper ships of old renown
　　Threescore long years ago!

Lion-Hearted

They had been strong, as those are strong who know neither doubts nor hopes. They had been impatient and enduring, turbulent and devoted, unruly and faithful. Well-meaning people had tried to represent those men as whining over every mouthful of their food; as going about their work in fear of their lives. But in truth they had been men who knew toil, privation, violence, debauchery—but knew not fear, and had no desire of spite in their hearts. Men hard to manage, but easy to inspire; voiceless men—but men enough to scorn in their hearts the sentimental voices that bewailed the hardness of their fate. It was a fate unique and their own; the capacity to bear it appeared to them the privilege of the chosen! Their generation lived inarticulate and indispensable, without knowing the sweetness of affections or the refuge of a home—and died free from the dark menace of a narrow grave. They were the everlasting children of the mysterious sea. Their successors are the grown-up children of a discontented earth. They are less naughty, but less innocent; less profane, but perhaps also less believing; and if they had learned how to speak they have also learned how to whine. But the others were strong and mute; they were effaced, bowed and enduring, like stone caryatids that hold up in the night the lighted halls of a resplendent and glorious edifice. They are gone now—and it does not matter. The sea and the earth are unfaithful to their children: a truth, a faith, a generation of men goes—and is forgotten, and it does not matter! Except, perhaps, to the few of those who believed the truth, confessed the faith—or loved the men.

Life-Force

FRANK VINING SMITH / JOSEPH CONRAD

Therein lies the secret of the seamen's special character as a body. The ship, this ship, our ship, the ship we serve, is the moral symbol of our life. A ship has to be respected, actually and ideally; her merit, her innocence, are sacred things. Of all the creations of man she is the closest partner of his toil and courage. From every point of view it is imperative that you should do well by her. And, as always in the case of true love, all you can do for her adds only to the tale of her merits in your heart. Mute and compelling, she claims not only your fidelity, but your respect. And the supreme "Well done!" which you may earn is made over to her.

. . .

It is my deep conviction, or, perhaps, I ought to say my deep feeling born from personal experience, that it is not the sea but the ships of the sea that guide and command that spirit of adventure which some say is the second nature of British men. I don't want to provoke a controversy (for intellectually I am rather a Quietist) but I venture to affirm that the main characteristic of the British men spread all over the world, is not the spirit of adventure so much as the spirit of service. I think that this could be demonstrated from the history of great voyages and the general activity of the race. That the British man has always liked his service to be adventurous rather than otherwise cannot be denied, for each British man began by being young in his time when all risk has a glamour. Afterwards, with the course of years, risk became a part of his daily work; he would have missed it from his side as one misses a loved companion.

The mere love of adventure is no saving grace. It is no grace at all. It lays a man under no obligation of faithfulness to an idea and even to his own self. Roughly speaking, an adventurer may be expected to have courage, or at any rate may be said to need it. But courage in itself is not an ideal. A successful highwayman showed courage of a sort, and pirate crews have been known to fight with courage or perhaps only with reckless desperation in the manner of cornered rats. There is nothing in the world to prevent a mere lover or pursuer of adventure from running at any moment. There is his own self, his mere taste for excitement, the prospect of some sort of gain, but there is no sort of loyalty to bind him in honour to consistent conduct. I have noticed that the majority of mere lovers of adventure are mightily careful of their skins; and the proof of it is that so many of them manage to keep it whole to an advanced age. You find them in mysterious nooks of islands and continents, mostly red-nosed and watery-eyed, and not even amusingly boastful. There is nothing more futile under the sun than a mere adventurer. He might have loved at one time—which would have been a saving grace. I mean loved adventure for itself. But if so, he was bound to lose this grace very soon. Adventure by itself is but a phantom, a dubious shape without a heart. Yes, there is nothing more futile than an adventurer, but nobody can say that the adventurous activities of the British race are stamped with the futility of a chase after mere emotions.

The successive generations that went out to sea from these Isles went out to toil desperately in adventurous conditions. A man is a worker. If he is not that he is nothing. Just nothing—like a mere adventurer. Those men understood the nature of their work, but more or less dimly, in various degrees of imperfection. The best and greatest of their leaders even had never seen it clearly, because of its magnitude and the remoteness of its end. This is the common fate of mankind, whose most positive achievements are born from dreams and visions followed loyally to an unknown destination. And it doesn't matter. For the great mass of mankind the only saving grace that is needed is steady fidelity to what is nearest to hand and heart in the short moment of each human effort. In other and in greater words, what is needed is a sense of immediate duty, and a feeling of impalpable constraint. Indeed, seamen and duty are all the time inseparable companions. It has been suggested to me that this sense of duty is not a patriotic sense or a religious sense, or even a social sense in a seaman. I don't know. It seems to me that a seaman's duty may be an unconscious compound of these three, something perhaps smaller than either, but something much more definite for the simple mind and more adapted to the humbleness of the seaman's task. It has been suggested also to me that this impalpable constraint is put upon the nature of a seaman by the Spirit of the Sea, which he serves with a dumb and dogged devotion.

Those are fine words conveying a fine idea. But this I do know, that it is very difficult to display a dogged devotion to a mere spirit, however great. In everyday life ordinary men require something much more material, effective, definite, and symbolic on which to concentrate their love and their devotion. And then, what is it, this Spirit of the Sea? It is too great and too elusive to be embraced and taken to a human breast. All that a guileless or guileful seaman knows of it is its hostility, its exaction of toil as endless as its ever-renewed horizons. No. What awakens the seaman's sense of duty, what lays that impalpable constraint upon the strength of his manliness, what commands his not always dumb if always dogged devotion, is not the spirit of the sea but something that in his eyes has a body, a character, a fascination, and almost a soul—it is his ship.

There is not a day that has passed for many centuries now without the sun seeing scattered over all the seas groups of British men whose material and moral existence is conditioned by their loyalty to each other and their faithful devotion to a ship.

The Good Navigator

· · ·

It hath appeared to me not out of order to do a little treatise on what is necessary to be a good and finished navigator, and on the qualifications that he should have. . . .

He should not allow himself to be overcome by wine; for when a captain or a mariner is a heavy drinker it is not well to entrust him with command or control, . . .

He should make the day his night and watch the greater part of the latter; always sleep clothed so as to be promptly on hand for accidents that may happen; keep his own private compass and often look at it to know if the course is being properly kept; and see that every member of the watch is doing his duty. . . .

He must be in readiness for ordinary dangers, be they fortuitous or through ignorance or rashness, getting you involved, as running before the wind onto a coast, doggedly trying to double a cape, or pursuing a hazardous course by night among banks, tidal flats, shoals, isles, rocks, or ice. . . .

He should be careful to keep the ship's reckoning, to know her point of departure, destination, position, where the land lies in relation to her, on what point of the wind; he should know what leeway she makes, and what she makes good on her course. He must never grow slack in these matters, which are a main source of errors; that is why, in all changes of wind and course, he should take great care to ascertain his position as near as possible, . . .

He should be a good celestial navigator, skilled in taking the altitude either with the cross-staff or the astrolabe, know the right ascension of the sun and its daily declination, in order to add or subtract [from the altitude], to take the altitude of the pole star with the cross-staff, take the bearing of the Guards. . . . and add to or subtract [from the altitude] the degrees they are above or below the pole star, according to the locality.

He should be able to recognize the Southern Cross when in south latitudes, add or subtract the degrees, recognize on occasion other stars if possible, so as to take their altitude when he loses sight of the former, or when he has not been able to take the sun's altitude owing to not seeing it precisely at noon. . . .

He should be experienced in pricking the chart correctly, to know if it is accurate according to the meridian where he is, if he can rely upon it, [and] how many leagues for each rhumb of the wind he must reckon for every higher degree. He should know the currents and tides and where they are to be met with, to properly enter the harbors and other places where he will have business, whether by day or night; and, if need be, he should be provided with good compasses and rutters for that object, and have seamen on the ship who know [those places], if by chance he has not himself been there; for sometimes the lives of the whole ship's company are saved by making use of these [currents and tides] in due time and place. . . .

To know how to make charts, so as to be able to recognize accurately the lie of the coast, entrances to ports, havens, roadsteads, rocks, shoals, reefs, islands, anchorages, capes, tidal currents, inlets, rivers, and streams with their heights and depths, the sea-marks and beacons on the edges of shoals, . . .

To know the Golden Number, the concurrent days of the year, the solar cycle, the dominical letter for each year, whether it is bissextile or not, the days on which the moon is in conjunction; on what day the months begin, how many days there are in each; the difference between the lunar and the solar year; the moon's age, how many degrees it traverses every day; what are the constellations of each month; how many leagues make a degree, north and south; how long the days are for each parallel of latitude, and how much shorter or longer they become every day; what are the hours of sunset and sunrise; what is the sun's daily declination, whether in the northern or the southern hemisphere; . . .

One thing in dead reckoning should never be forgotten—to overestimate rather than underestimate the distance traversed; for instance, if the vessel seems to make two leagues an hour, give her one-eighth or more in addition, according to the distance covered by the reckoning and the length of the voyage; for it is better to be twenty leagues behind than too soon ahead, in which case one might find oneself ashore or in danger of shipwreck. . . . If soundings are to be had off one's destination, one should begin to heave the lead a day earlier rather than later; and if having done so, one expects to find bottom, keep on heaving it every watch during the night or in fog. This is the way to avoid danger, for one cannot be too apprehensive of what one would not like to see, particularly since you cannot make that mistake twice. . . .

The Honor of Labor

Now, the moral side of an industry, productive or unproductive, the redeeming and ideal aspect of this bread-winning, is the attainment and preservation of the highest possible skill on the part of the craftsmen. Such skill, the skill of technique, is more than honesty; it is something wider, embracing honesty and grace and rule in an elevated and clear sentiment, not altogether utilitarian, which may be called the honour of labour. It is made up of accumulated tradition, kept alive by individual pride, rendered exact by professional opinion, and, like the higher arts, it is spurred on and sustained by discriminating praise.

This is why the attainment of proficiency, the pushing of your skill with attention to the most delicate shades of excellence, is a matter of vital concern. Efficiency of a practically flawless kind may be reached naturally in the struggle for bread. But there is something beyond—a higher point, a subtle and unmistakable touch of love and pride beyond mere skill; almost an inspiration which gives to all work that finish which is almost art—which *is* art.

Master Mariners

The names of the clipper ship captains have gone down on the log of the sea with the names of their ships, an imperishable scroll. Gardner of the *Celestial*, Hollis of the *Game Cock*, Stoddard of the *Mandarin*, King of the *Racehorse*, Richardson of the *Stag-hound*, Farran of the *Eagle*; Dumaresq, one of the greatest seamen, commanded the following clippers—*Surprise*, *Bald Eagle*, *Romance of the Seas*, *Florence*; Miller of the *Dauntless*; G. B. Waterman of the *Highflyer*; the more famous Robert H. Waterman of the clippers *Britannia*, *Natchez*, *Sea Witch*, *Northerner* and *Challenge*. Captain Bob Waterman was a young shipmaster of unusually attractive personality, noted for his ability as a seaman and navigator, and for his power of command and discipline, a quality very necessary on a long voyage with hard-case crews and large numbers of strange passengers. Once, when serving on the *Britannia*, one of the sailors fell from aloft during a heavy gale. Bob Waterman dived into the sea and saved the man's life at the risk of his own. He was presented with a substantial testimonial by the passengers for his heroic act. He was then mate, and two years later was given command. He hung up many records as a seaman and made five voyages around the globe.

Then we must note Captain Lauchlan McKay, brother of the great ship builder, whose first command was the *Jenny Lind*. In his forty-first year he was a man of robust build, of exceptional attainments, a seaman of culture, and the author of a work on naval architecture when he attained command of that beautiful ship *The Sovereign of the Seas*.

A few more clipper captains might be mentioned—Limeburner of the *Flying Cloud*, Asa Eldridge of the *Red Jacket*, who made the fastest passage between Sandy Hook and the Rock Light, off the Port of Liverpool in thirteen days, one hour in 1854. This latter passage was of significant interest in that stirring contest between the fastest ships of sail and the early ships of steam.

A Collins Line steamer, which left New York two days before the *Red Jacket*, arrived in Liverpool on Sunday afternoon and brought news that a Yankee Clipper was just astern. Those were sporting days. There was intense interest in the performance of ships. When the news spread along the Liverpool waterfront people rushed in thousands to the docks; every vantage point was black with spectators awaiting the arrival of this incredible racer. Outside the port tugs had offered to tow the clipper, but she was going so fast they never could have kept their hawsers taut. She shot ahead, leaving them puffing and wallowing in her wake. The *Red Jacket* swept into the Mersey with everything drawing, presenting a spectacle of surpassing grandeur. Cheers burst from the thousands on the shore. The captain, Asa Eldridge, gave them a thrill they had least expected—he took in his kites, his skysails, royals and topgallants, hung his courses or lower sails, ignored the tugs that caught up and, throwing the *Red Jacket* into the wind, helm hard down, he backed her alongside of the berth without aid, while the crew took in sail with a celerity that seemed like magic to the spectators—a superb piece of seamanship!

A high degree of daring entered into the handling of the clip-pers, daring bred of skill, and necessary if passage expectations were to be fulfilled. Almost any good seaman can carry on during the day, but at night, when the wind is high, sea lively, squalls always liable to sweep across the ship, seamanship and nerve must side with the command. The captains never turned in except "all standing" as the saying goes—that is fully dressed. What sleep they got was fitful and insecure. In stormy or thick weather they might not be out of their clothes for days on end. The officers led a life scarcely less rigorous, and crews, standing watches of four on and four off, were expected to tumble out at a moment's notice with the stirring call of "All hands on deck." It was a tense, exciting game. The clippers sped along with lee scuppers awash, hands at the halliards, the more important ropes being racked to prevent some weak ones from letting to when a squall bore them down and the singing wind and humming ropes and sails seemed to spell the end. At such times the "old man" was in supreme command and would stand on the high weather side of the poop, controlling the mountainous piles of canvas and defying the wind, using it to the utmost in the struggle for speed. Men have never since quite equalled this heroic art of sailing. Fast as we are, it is through machinery and not by the uncertain wind, the white squall, the rip of lightning, the roar of the sea, and the command of the tiller and gear and men that went with the rushing progress of the clipper ship.

Sea-Fever

I must go down to the seas again, to the lonely sea and the sky,
And all I ask is a tall ship and a star to steer her by,
And the wheel's kick and the wind's song and the white sail's shaking,
And a grey mist on the sea's face and a grey dawn breaking.

I must go down to the seas again, for the call of the running tide
Is a wild call and a clear call that may not be denied;
And all I ask is a windy day with the white clouds flying,
And the flung spray and the blown spume, and the sea-gulls crying.

I must go down to the seas again to the vagrant gypsy life,
To the gull's way and the whale's way where the wind's
   like a whetted knife;
And all I ask is a merry yarn from a laughing fellow-rover,
And quiet sleep and a sweet dream when the long trick's over.

Acknowledgments

Full credits for all art and literature appearing in the book are listed below, page by page; in cases where visual and textual material appear on the same page, the illustration credit is given first and the entries are separated by a slash.

PAGE

1. George Gale, *Foretop.* Courtesy Mary D. Gale
2. Howard Pyle, *Old Man with Bowl.* Courtesy Delaware Art Museum, Wilmington/Algernon Charles Swinburne, from "The Triumph of Time"
3. Dwight C. Sturges, *Gloucester Fisherman*
5. Gordon Grant, *The Man at the Wheel.* Courtesy Seamen's Bank for Savings, Fine Arts Collection
6. Frank W. Benson, *Launching Dory.* Courtesy Library of Congress
7. Gordon Grant, *Eight Bells*
8. George C. Wales, *The Old Port.* Courtesy Boston Public Library, Print Department
9. Edwin James Brady, from "You and Us," in *The Ways of Many Waters.* Courtesy Bulletin Newspaper Company, Sydney, Australia; Samuel Eliot Morison, from *The Oxford History of the American People.* Oxford University Press
10. Edward Hopper, *The Cat Boat.* Courtesy New York Public Library, Astor, Lenox and Tilden Foundations, Prints Division
11. Samuel Eliot Morison, in Emily Morison Beck, ed., *Sailor Historian: The Best of Samuel Eliot Morison.* Houghton Mifflin Company and Curtis Brown Ltd.
12. Arthur Briscoe, *The Pilot.* Courtesy Amherst College, Crossett Collection/Kenneth Grahame, from *The Wind in the Willows*
13. George C. Wales, *Away You Rio.* Courtesy Boston Public Library, Print Department
14. Samuel Emery, *Mariner's Compass Rose Card.* Courtesy Peabody Museum of Salem
15. George Chapman, "The Master Spirit," from *The Conspiracy of Charles, Duke of Byron*
16. John Masefield, "Roadways." Macmillan Publishing Co., Inc., and The Society of Authors
17. Franklin Booth, *Harbor in the Morning*
18. James A. McNeill-Whistler, *Rotherhithe.* Courtesy New York Public Library, Astor, Lenox and Tilden Foundations, Prints Division
19. Unknown, from "Sir Richard Grenville's Farewell"
20. Henry Wadsworth Longfellow, from "The Building of the Ship"
21. Anders Zorn, *Zorn and His Wife.* Courtesy Boston Public Library, Print Department
22. Frank Brangwyn, *Sawyers.* Courtesy New York Public Library, Astor, Lenox and Tilden Foundations, Prints Division/Henry Wadsworth Longfellow, from "The Building of the Ship"
23. George Gale, *The Shipyard*/Henry Wadsworth Longfellow, from "The Building of the Ship"
24. Henry Wadsworth Longfellow, from "The Building of the Ship"
25. Howard Pyle, *In the Woodcarver's Shop.* Courtesy Delaware Art Museum, Wilmington
26. Henry Wadsworth Longfellow, from "The Building of the Ship"
27. Arthur Briscoe, *Painting the Main Mast.* Courtesy Boston Public Library, Print Department
28. Unknown, *Boston Shipyard.* Courtesy Peabody Museum of Salem
29. Henry Wadsworth Longfellow, from "The Building of the Ship"
30. George Gale, *Top High Water*/John Masefield, "A Wanderer's Song." Macmillan Publishing Co., Inc., and The Society of Authors
31. George Gale, *Waterfront Loafers.* Courtesy Mary D. Gale
32. John Masefield, from "A Ballad of John Silver." Macmillan Publishing Co., Inc., and The Society of Authors
33. James A. McNeill Whistler, *Longshoremen.* Courtesy New York Public Library, Astor, Lenox and Tilden Foundations, Prints Division, S. P. Avery Collection
34–35. Richard H. Rodgers, seven sketches from *Deep Water Days,* Oliver G. Swan, ed. Macrae Smith Company/John Masefield, from "A Ballad of John Silver." Macmillan Publishing Co., Inc., and The Society of Authors
36. John Masefield, from "A Ballad of John Silver." Macmillan Publishing Co., Inc., and The Society of Authors
37. Howard Pyle, *Walking the Plank*
38. George Gale, *Sailing Day.* Courtesy Nancy A. Warden
39. Rudyard Kipling, "The Sea-Wife." Doubleday & Company, Inc., and A. P. Watt & Son
40. Arthur Briscoe, *We're Bound for Rio Grande.* Courtesy Herbert W. Warden, IV
41. Unknown, "Rio Grande," capstan chantey
42. George Gale, *Towing Out*
43. John Masefield, from "The Setting Forth," in *The Wanderer of Liverpool.* Macmillan Publishing Co., Inc., and The Society of Authors
44. John Masefield, from "The Setting Forth," in *The Wanderer of Liverpool.* Macmillan Publishing Co., Inc., and The Society of Authors
45. John Stobart, *South Street Piers in the 1890's.* Courtesy the artist and Kennedy Galleries, Inc., N.Y.
46. Anton Otto Fischer, *Outward Bound.* Courtesy Katrina Sigsbee Fischer
47. Joseph Conrad, from *The Nigger of the "Narcissus"*
48. Joseph Conrad, from *The Nigger of the "Narcissus"*
49. John Stobart, *The Gatherer.* Courtesy the artist and Kennedy Galleries, Inc., N.Y.
50. Allan Cunningham, "A Wet Sheet and a Flowing Sea"
51. Arthur Briscoe, *Furling the Foresail*
52. Montague Dawson, *Masts Against the Sky.* Courtesy Mariners Museum of Newport News, Va., and Frost & Reed Ltd., England
53. Joseph Conrad, from *The Mirror of the Sea*
54. Joseph Conrad, from *The Mirror of the Sea*
55. Arthur Briscoe, *Our Bow.* Courtesy Boston Public Library, Print Department
56. Gordon Grant, *The Helmsman*
57. Rudyard Kipling, from "The Nurses." Doubleday & Company, Inc., and A. P. Watt & Son
58. Gordon Grant, *The Skipper Takes a Sight*
59. John Paul Jones, quoted in Lt. Comdr. Leland P. Lovette, USN, *Naval Customs, Traditions, and Usage;* John Ross Browne, from *Etchings of a Whaling Cruise*
60. Washington Irving, from *A Transatlantic Voyage in 1815*
61. George C. Wales, *Fog.* Courtesy Boston Public Library, Print Department
62. Gordon Grant, *Signaling*
63. Don Blanding, from *Names Are Ships.* Dodd, Mead & Company
64. Gordon Grant, *A Dog Watch Concert*
65. Gordon Grant, *Song Birds*/Frederick Marryat, "The Captain Stood on the Carronade"
66. Gordon Grant, *Heaving the Lead*/Charles Dibdin, from "The Leadman's Song," adapted by Herbert W. Warden, III
67. William H. Drury, *Mt. Road, Dominique, Roseau River.* Courtesy the family of the artist
68. Charles Dibdin, from "The Leadman's Song"
69. Jack Spurling, *Old Kensington.* Courtesy Calendars of Distinction, Ltd.
70. Philip Kappel, *Off Shore, West Indies.* Courtesy the artist
71. Gordon Grant, *Bumboats*/Herbert W. Warden, III, *Bumboats*
72. William H. Drury, *Rose.* Courtesy the family of the artist
73. Philip Kappel, *Lobsterman at Dawn.* Courtesy the artist and Anne H. Warden/John Masefield, from "Trade Winds." Macmillan Publishing Co., Inc., and The Society of Authors
74. John Masefield, "A Night at Dago Tom's." Macmillan Publishing Co., Inc., and The Society of Authors
75. Henri de Toulouse-Lautrec, *Terreur de Grenelle.* Courtesy William Weston Gallery Ltd., London
76. Rufus F. Zogbaum, *Oars*
77. Felix Riesenberg, Sr., from *Living Again, An Autobiography.* Courtesy Felix Riesenberg III
78. Gordon Grant, *The Bucko Mate*
79. John Masefield, "Evening–Regatta Day." Macmillan Publishing Co., Inc., and The Society of Authors
80. Robert W. Service, from "The Ballad of How MacPherson Held the Floor." Dodd, Mead & Company, McGraw-Hill Ryerson Ltd., and Ernest Benn Ltd.
81. George Gale, *Hell Afloat*
82. George Gale, *Viola Just Arrived*
83. John Masefield, "Fever Ship." Macmillan Publishing Co., Inc., and The Society of Authors
84. Frank E. Schoonover, *The Sloop Dropped Anchor.* Courtesy private collection
85. John Masefield, "Spanish Waters." Macmillan Publishing Co., Inc., and The Society of Authors
86. Howard Pyle, *Kidd at Gardiner's Island.* Courtesy Fenn Galleries, Santa Fe, N. Mex.
87. George Varian, *Pirate with Monkey,* from *The Great Quest* by Charles Boardman Hawes. Little, Brown and Company/John Masefield, "Spanish Waters." Macmillan Publishing Co., Inc., and The Society of Authors
88. Rudyard Kipling, from "The Last Lap." Doubleday & Company, Inc., and A. P. Watt & Son
89. George C. Wales, *Morning Mist.* Courtesy Boston Public Library, Print Department
90. Guenther T. Schulz, *The Anchor Is Up.* Courtesy Koehlers Verlagsgesellschaft MBH/John Masefield, from "A Valediction." Macmillan Publishing Co., Inc., and The Society of Authors
91. Gordon Grant, *A Pull on the Lee Fore Braces*
92. George Gale, *Bousing down the Foretack*
93. Frederick L. Owen, *Deep Sea Harmony*/John Masefield, from "A Valediction." Macmillan Publishing Co., Inc., and The Society of Authors
94. Gordon Grant, *Heading for Port.* Courtesy Associated American Artists, N.Y.
95. John Masefield, from "Cape Horn Gospel—I." Macmillan Publishing Co., Inc., and The Society of Authors
96. Gordon Grant, *The Foc's'le*/Felix Riesenberg, Sr., from *Under Sail.* Courtesy Felix Riesenberg III
97. Gordon Grant, *Crossing the Line*/Felix Riesenberg, Sr., from *Under Sail.* Courtesy Felix Riesenberg III
98. Gordon Grant, *Bathing in the Rain*
99. Anton Otto Fischer, from *Foc's'le Days.* Courtesy Katrina Sigsbee Fischer
100. John Masefield, from *Tarpaulin Muster.* The Society of Authors
101. John F. Leavitt, *Panay.* Courtesy Peabody Museum of Salem
102. Josiah P. Cressy, Master of the "Flying Cloud," from *Log of New York to San Francisco Voyage, 1851*
103. Hydrographic map, from Cape Horn to the Magellan Strait, 1874. Courtesy Library of Congress
104. Guenther T. Schulz, *Fog Horn.* Courtesy Koehlers Verlagsgesellschaft MBH
105. John Masefield, from "Dauber." Macmillan Publishing Co., Inc., and The Society of Authors
106. John Masefield, from "Dauber." Macmillan Publishing Co., Inc., and The Society of Authors
107. Winslow Homer, *Eight Bells.* Courtesy New York Public Library, Astor, Lenox and Tilden Foundations, Prints Division
108. George C. Wales, *The Squall.* Courtesy Boston Public Library, Print Department/John Masefield, from "Dauber." Macmillan Publishing Co., Inc., and The Society of Authors
109. Gordon Grant, *All Hands*
110. Arthur Briscoe, *The Main Rigging.* Courtesy Mary Warden Taylor
111. John Masefield, from "Dauber." Macmillan Publishing Co., Inc., and The Society of Authors
112. Montague Dawson, *The Rising Wind.* Courtesy Frost & Reed Ltd., England
113. John Masefield, from "Dauber." Macmillan

Publishing Co., Inc., and The Society of Authors

114. John Masefield, from "Dauber." Macmillan Publishing Co., Inc., and The Society of Authors

115. Lyle Galloway, Who Wouldn't Sell the Farm to Go to Sea? Courtesy the artist

116. Lyle Galloway, Fisting the Frozen Crojick. Courtesy the artist

117. John Masefield, from "Dauber." Macmillan Publishing Co., Inc., and The Society of Authors

118. John Masefield, from "Dauber." Macmillan Publishing Co., Inc., and The Society of Authors

119. Arthur Briscoe, Flooded Decks. Courtesy Boston Public Library, Print Department

120. Lyle Galloway, Coiling Down. Courtesy the artist

121. John Masefield, from "Dauber." Macmillan Publishing Co., Inc., and The Society of Authors

122. Frank Hubert Shaw, from White Sails and Spindrift (abridged)

123. William Edward Norton, Unidentified American Brig in Distress. Courtesy Peabody Museum of Salem

124. Arthur Briscoe, Man Overboard

125. Frank Hubert Shaw, from White Sails and Spindrift (abridged)

126. Anton Otto Fischer, Worsening Weather. Courtesy U.S. Coast Guard Museum, New London, Conn./Frank Hubert Shaw, from White Sails and Spindrift (abridged)

127. Gordon Grant, The Wreck Rose up on a Crest/Frank Hubert Shaw, from White Sails and Spindrift (abridged)

128. Frank Hubert Shaw, from White Sails and Spindrift (abridged)

129. H. W. Ditzler, A Rescue. Courtesy The Mariner's Catalog, Peter H. Spectre and George Putz, eds. International Marine Publishing Co., Camden, Maine

130. Frank Hubert Shaw, from White Sails and Spindrift (abridged)

131. Winslow Homer, The Last Boat In. Courtesy Addison Gallery of American Art, Phillips Academy, Andover, Mass.

132. Frank Hubert Shaw, from White Sails and Spindrift (abridged)

133. Marshall Johnson, Benares. Courtesy Peabody Museum of Salem

134. Dwight C. Sturges, Gloucester Fisherman

135. Walt Whitman, from "Song for All Seas, All Ships"

136. Gordon Grant, The Sailmaker/C. Fox Smith, "Sails." Methuen & Co. Ltd.

137. Gordon Grant, Holystoning/C. Fox Smith, "Rolling Stone." Methuen & Co. Ltd.

138. Gordon Grant, Words with the Cook

139. Herman Melville, from Omoo

140. John P. Benson, Whaling Scene. Courtesy Peabody Museum of Salem

141. Gordon Grant, The Masthead/John Ross Browne, from Etchings of a Whaling Cruise

142. Gordon Grant, Lowering

143. George Gale, Boats Away/John Ross Browne, from Etchings of a Whaling Cruise; Washington Chase, from A Voyage from the United States to South America Performed

During the Years 1821, 1822 and 1823

144. George Gale, Harpooner

145. George Gale, The "Live" Iron/Washington Chase, from A Voyage from the United States to South America Performed During the Years 1821, 1822 and 1823

146. George Gale, "Fast" Boat

147. George Gale, Haul Line/Herman Melville, from Moby Dick

148. Herman Melville, from Moby Dick

149. George Gale, Fighting Whale

150. William Gilkerson, Sperm Whale Jimmy Directing His Boats. Courtesy the artist/Herman Melville, from Moby Dick

151. Gordon Grant, A Breach

152. Lyle Galloway, Sailor's Delight. Courtesy the artist

153. Robert N. Rose, "My Ship o' Dreams"

154. S. W. Williams, Map of city of Canton and adjacent islands, 1847. Courtesy New York Public Library, Astor, Lenox and Tilden Foundations, Map Division

155. Robert Carse, from The Moonrakers. Harper & Row, Publishers

156. Unknown Chinese artist, Levant and Milo. Courtesy Peabody Museum of Salem

157. Robert Carse, from The Moonrakers. Harper & Row, Publishers

158. Robert Carse, from The Moonrakers. Harper & Row, Publishers

159. Unknown Chinese artist, Macao Passage near Canton. Courtesy Peabody Museum of Salem (The actual Bogue forts were similar architecturally to the one portrayed but were on steeper ground.)

160. Robert Carse, from The Moonrakers. Harper & Row, Publishers

161. Unknown Chinese artist, China, Whampoa Anchorage. Courtesy Peabody Museum of Salem

162. George Chinnery, Sampan, Cows, Calves, People (detail) and Three Figures Mending a Garment for a Sailor. Both courtesy Peabody Museum of Salem/Robert Carse, from The Moonrakers. Harper & Row, Publishers

163. George Chinnery, Macao, Figures Poling Sampan. Courtesy Peabody Museum of Salem/Robert Carse, from The Moonrakers. Harper & Row, Publishers

164. Unknown Chinese artist, Harvest Boat, Dutch Folly Fort, Canton in Distance. Courtesy Peabody Museum of Salem/Robert Carse, from The Moonrakers. Harper & Row, Publishers

165. James A. McNeill Whistler, sketch for Variations in Flesh Color & Green–The Balcony. Courtesy New York Public Library, Astor, Lenox and Tilden Foundations, Prints Division/Robert Carse, from The Moonrakers. Harper & Row, Publishers

166. Robert Carse, from The Moonrakers. Harper & Row, Publishers

167. Unknown Chinese artist, Canton. Courtesy Peabody Museum of Salem

168. Edmund Blampied, The Cider Drinkers. Courtesy Mrs. Edmund Blampied, and Madison (Wis.) Art Center, gift of Mrs. Charles Bunn

169. John Masefield, from "Captain Stratton's Fancy." Macmillan Publishing Co., Inc., and

The Society of Authors

170. George Chinnery, Macao, Seagoing Junk, 1838. Courtesy Peabody Museum of Salem

171. Rudyard Kipling, "The Junk and the Dhow." Doubleday & Company, Inc., and A. P. Watt & Son

172. Montague Dawson, The Thermopylae Leaving Foochow. Courtesy Frost & Reed Ltd., England

173. C. Fox Smith, "By the Old Pagoda Anchorage." Methuen & Co. Ltd.

174. Arthur Briscoe, The Anchor. Courtesy Amherst College, Crossett Collection

175. Herman Melville, from Moby Dick

176. Walter Mitchell, "Tacking Ship Off Shore"

177. Arthur Briscoe, The Binnacle. Courtesy Boston Public Library, Print Department

178–79. William Gilkerson, American Merchantman Under Attack by Malayan Pirate Praus. Courtesy the artist/Frederic Stanhope Hill, from Twenty Years at Sea, or Leaves from My Old Log Books (abridged)

180. Guenther T. Schulz, Sailorizing Jobs. Courtesy Koehlers Verlagsgesellschaft MBH

181. Herman Melville, from Redburn

182. William Lee-Hankey, The Betrothal. Courtesy William Weston Gallery Ltd., London

183. John Masefield, "Third Mate." Macmillan Publishing Co., Inc., and The Society of Authors

184. Frank Hubert Shaw, from White Sails and Spindrift (abridged)

185. Arthur Briscoe, Command. Courtesy Amherst College, Crossett Collection

186. Anton Otto Fischer, Running Before the Gale. Courtesy Katrina Sigsbee Fischer/Frank Hubert Shaw, from White Sails and Spindrift (abridged)

187. Frank Hubert Shaw, from White Sails and Spindrift (abridged)

188. Frank Hubert Shaw, from White Sails and Spindrift (abridged)

189. Gordon Grant, Two Men at the Wheel/Frank Hubert Shaw, White Sails and Spindrift (abridged)

190. Guenther T. Schulz, Man Overboard. Courtesy Koehlers Verlagsgesellschaft MBH

191. John Masefield, "One of Wally's Yarns." Macmillan Publishing Co., Inc., and The Society of Authors

192. John Masefield, "Sea-Change." Macmillan Publishing Co., Inc., and The Society of Authors

193. Stanley Rogers, On the Bowsprit, from his book The Sailing Ship. Harper & Row, Publishers

194. Gordon Grant, Old Windjammer. Courtesy Mariners Museum of Newport News, Va., and Associated American Artists, N.Y.

195. Anton Otto Fischer, Land Ho! Courtesy Katrina Sigsbee Fischer/Herman Melville, from Typee

196. John Masefield, "Campeachy Picture." Macmillan Publishing Co., Inc., and The Society of Authors

197. Philip Kappel, West Indian Grandeur. Courtesy the artist

198. Gordon Grant, Recruiting on the Beach

199. Don Blanding, from "How to Know Hawaii." Dodd, Mead & Company

200. Herman Melville, from Moby Dick

201. Winslow Homer, Palm Tree, Nassau. Courtesy Metropolitan Museum of Art, N.Y., Lazarus Fund, 1910

202. Unknown, "We're Homeward Bound," capstan chantey

203. Gordon Grant, The Capstan. Courtesy Seamen's Bank for Savings, Fine Arts Collection

204. Anton Otto Fischer, Scrimmage at Sea. Courtesy Little, Brown and Company

205. Herman Melville, from White-Jacket

206. John Masefield, from Tarpaulin Muster. The Society of Authors

207. Frank Vining Smith, Ship Ahoy. Courtesy Seamen's Bank for Savings, Fine Arts Collection

208. Henry Howard Brownell, "The Burial of the Dane"

209. Anton Otto Fischer, Burial at Sea. Courtesy Katrina Sigsbee Fischer

210. Winslow Homer, The Wrecked Schooner. Courtesy The St. Louis Art Museum/John Masefield, "Sing a Song o' Shipwreck." Macmillan Publishing Co., Inc., and The Society of Authors

211. George Gale, The Stove Boat. Courtesy Kendall Whaling Museum, Sharon, Mass./John Masefield, "Sing a Song o' Shipwreck." Macmillan Publishing Co., Inc., and The Society of Authors

212. Richard Henry Dana, Jr., from Two Years Before the Mast

213. Frederick E. Church, The Iceberg. Courtesy Museum of Art, Carnegie Institute, Pittsburgh, Pa.

214. David Bone, from "After Forty Year," in The Brassbounder. E. P. Dutton & Co. and Gerald Duckworth & Co. Ltd.

215. Anton Otto Fischer, Misty Marine with Gulls. Courtesy Katrina Sigsbee Fischer

216. David Bone, from "After Forty Year," in The Brassbounder. E. P. Dutton & Co. and Gerald Duckworth & Co. Ltd.

217. William Gilkerson, Whaler "California" in Ice and Mist. Courtesy the artist

218. Guenther T. Schulz, The Fore Topmast Carried away in a Hard Squall. Courtesy Koehlers Verlagsgesellschaft MBH

219. David Bone, from "After Forty Year," in The Brassbounder. E. P. Dutton & Co. and Gerald Duckworth & Co. Ltd.

220. Norman Wilkinson, The Roaring Forties. Courtesy Amherst College, Crossett Collection

221. Joseph Conrad, from The Mirror of the Sea

222. Joseph Conrad, from The Nigger of the "Narcissus"

223. Anton Otto Fischer, Lee Braces. Courtesy Katrina Sigsbee Fischer

224. Barry Moser, Captain Allistoun (reproduced in reverse). Courtesy the artist/Joseph Conrad, from The Nigger of the "Narcissus"

225. Barry Moser, Hanging On. Courtesy the artist/Joseph Conrad, from The Nigger of the "Narcissus"

226. Joseph Conrad, from The Nigger of the "Narcissus"

227. Arthur Briscoe, All Hands. Courtesy Boston Public Library, Print Department

228. Anton Otto Fischer, The Gwydyr Castle.

Courtesy Katrina Sigsbee Fischer/Joseph Conrad, from *The Nigger of the "Narcissus"*

229. Joseph Conrad, from *The Nigger of the "Narcissus"*
230. Joseph Conrad, from *The Nigger of the "Narcissus"*
231. Arthur Briscoe, *Stowing the Mainsail.* Courtesy Amherst College, Crossett Collection
232. Gordon Grant, *Swaying Off*/Joseph Conrad, from *The Nigger of the "Narcissus"*
233. Frank Vining Smith, *Turbulence at Sea.* Courtesy Seamen's Church Institute of New York
234. Lyle Galloway, *Main Tops'l Halyard.* Courtesy the artist
235. Felix Riesenberg, Sr., from *Under Sail.* Courtesy Felix Riesenberg III
236. John Stobart, *Aboard Cutty Sark Decks.* Courtesy the artist and Kennedy Galleries, Inc., N.Y.
237. C. Fox Smith, "What the Old Man Said." Methuen & Co. Ltd.
238. Warren Sheppard, *Young America.* Courtesy Addison Gallery of American Art, Phillips Academy, Andover, Mass./Tom Manners, "Crack It On You Bullies," from *Song of the Seas and Tall Ships—Collection of Sea Ballads.* Murray & Gee
239. Tom Manners, "Crack It On You Bullies," from *Song of the Seas and Tall Ships—Collection of Sea Ballads.* Murray & Gee
240. Guenther T. Schulz, *The Muster.* Courtesy Koehlers Verlagsgesellschaft MBH
241. John Masefield. "Eight Bells." Macmillan Publishing Co., Inc., and The Society of Authors.
242. Richard Henry Dana, Jr., from *Two Years Before the Mast*
243. Guenther T. Schulz, *The Look-out in the Forecastle Head.* Courtesy Koehlers Verlagsgesellschaft MBH
244. Guenther T. Schulz, *Saturday Afternoon Scrub Down.* Courtesy Koehlers Verlagsgesellschaft MBH/Richard Henry Dana, Jr., from *Two Years Before the Mast*
245. Gordon Grant, *Mending Clothes*/Richard Henry Dana, Jr., from *Two Years Before the Mast*
246. Richard Henry Dana, Jr., from *Two Years Before the Mast*
247. Philip Little, *Square Riggers in the Tropics.* Courtesy Childs Gallery, Boston
248. George Gale, *Bending the Lower Tops'l*
249. George Gale, *Caulk and Pay.* Courtesy Mary D. Gale/Richard Henry Dana, Jr., from *Two Years Before the Mast*
250. Joseph Conrad, from *The Nigger of the "Narcissus"*
251. Michael F. Blaser, *The Flying Cloud.* Courtesy the artist
252. Joseph Conrad, from *The Nigger of the "Narcissus"*
253. James G. Tyler, *Lighthouse in the Moonlight.* Courtesy private collection
254. George C. Wales, *J.D.* Courtesy Boston Public Library, Print Department (Buoy illustrated is not a bell buoy.)
255. Rudyard Kipling, "The Bell Buoy." Doubleday & Company, Inc., and A. P. Watt & Son

256. Samuel Eliot Morison, in Emily Morison Beck, ed., *Sailor Historian: The Best of Samuel Eliot Morison.* Houghton Mifflin Company and Curtis Brown Ltd.
257. Frank Vining Smith, *Full-Rigged Ship with Stun Sails.* Courtesy Kennedy Galleries, Inc., N.Y.
258. Philip Kappel, *Curiosity.* Courtesy the artist/Samuel Eliot Morison, in Emily Morison Beck, ed., *Sailor Historian: The Best of Samuel Eliot Morison.* Houghton Mifflin Company and Curtis Brown Ltd.
259. William Gilkerson, *Getting in the Main.* Courtesy the artist/Samuel Eliot Morison, in Emily Morison Beck, ed., *Sailor Historian: The Best of Samuel Eliot Morison.* Houghton Mifflin Company and Curtis Brown Ltd.
260. Samuel Eliot Morison, in Emily Morison Beck, ed., *Sailor Historian: The Best of Samuel Eliot Morison.* Houghton Mifflin Company and Curtis Brown Ltd.
261. Arthur Briscoe, *Mooring Her.* Courtesy Amherst College, Crossett Collection
262. John Masefield, "The Crowd," from *The Wanderer of Liverpool,* Macmillan Publishing Co., Inc., and The Society of Authors
263. Gordon Grant, *Leaving Her*
264. George Gale, *Four-Footed Stevedores*/John Masefield, "The Wanderer," from *The Wanderer of Liverpool.* Macmillan Publishing Co., Inc., and The Society of Authors
265. George Gale, *Discharging the Oil*
266. William H. Drury, *A Sword Fisher.* Courtesy the family of the artist
267. Rudyard Kipling, "The Sea and the Hills." Doubleday & Company, Inc., and A. P. Watt & Son
268. Robert Browning, "Meeting at Night"
269. Frank W. Benson, *Bound Home.* Courtesy Library of Congress
270. William Lee-Hankey, *Étaples Fisher Folk*
271. Rudyard Kipling, "My Boy Jack." Doubleday & Company, Inc., and A. P. Watt & Son
272. Daniel Whitehead Hicky, "Who Pilots Ships," from *Bright Harbor.* Holt, Rinehart and Winston
273. Philip Kappel, *Off the Grand Banks.* Courtesy the artist
274. John Stobart, *South Street, New York, in 1880, by Gaslight.* Courtesy the artist and Maritime Heritage Prints, Inc., Washington, D.C.
275. John Masefield, from "Ships." Macmillan Publishing Co., Inc., and The Society of Authors
276. C. Fox Smith, "The Old Breed." Methuen & Co. Ltd.
277. Philip Kappel, *Old Love.* Courtesy the artist
278. Joseph Conrad, from *The Nigger of the "Narcissus"*
279. Winslow Homer, *The Lookout—All's Well.* Courtesy Museum of Fine Arts, Boston, William Wilkins Warren Fund
280. Frank Vining Smith, *Crew Manning Sail.* Courtesy Seamen's Church Institute of New York
281. Joseph Conrad, "Well Done," from *Joseph Conrad: Life and Letters* by Jean-Aubry. Doubleday & Company, Inc.

282. George Gale, *The Old Timer.* Courtesy Mary D. Gale
283. Samuel Eliot Morison, from *Samuel de Champlain: Father of New France.* Little, Brown and Company
284. Joseph Conrad, from *The Mirror of the Sea*
285. George Gale, *Weathering the Headland.* Courtesy Mary D. Gale
286. Muirhead Bone, *Portrait of Joseph Conrad.* Courtesy Boston Public Library, Print Department/Felix Riesenberg, Sr., from *Clipper Ships.* Courtesy Felix Riesenberg III
287. Felix Riesenberg, Sr., from *Clipper Ships.* Courtesy Felix Riesenberg III
288. John Masefield, "Sea-Fever." Macmillan Publishing Co., Inc., and The Society of Authors
289. Philip Kappel, *Ghosting Along.* Courtesy the artist
293. Richard H. Barham, from *Ingoldsby Legends*
296. Robert G. Herbert, Jr., Sail plan and rigging of a ship
298. Kerr Eby, *Woman Waving Goodbye from Widow's Walk.* Courtesy *The Mariner's Catalog,* Peter H. Spectre and George Putz, eds. International Marine Publishing Co., Camden, Maine/Joseph Conrad, Letter to owners and crew of the "Tusitala," dated June 2, 1923. Courtesy Seamen's Church Institute of New York

My special thanks go to the hard-working crew whose collective efforts made this book possible: Alexandria Hatcher, literary agent; Arthur Levine of Washington, D.C., and David C. J. Brown and Laurence J. Cohen of London, copyright attorneys; Barbara Zimmerman, rights and permissions director; Jane S. Hart, administrative coordinator; and Robert G. Herbert, Jr., marine historian.

At Harry N. Abrams, Inc., I am indebted to Robert Morton for his belief in this book and his perseverance; Margaret Donovan for her exceptional editorial assistance; Jos. Trautwein for the handsome design; and Christine Murphy, Barbara Lyons, Nai Chang, Marion Newman, and Peg Streep for their individual help and expertise.

These contemporary artists have most kindly permitted me to use their work: Michael F. Blaser, Philip Kappel, Lyle Galloway, William Gilkerson, Barry Moser, and John Stobart. Katrina S. Fischer, Mary D. Gale, Howard Pyle Brokaw, Mrs. Courtland Schoonover, and the family of William H. Drury were immensely helpful in locating many important paintings, etchings, and drawings.

I have drawn heavily on the staffs and resources of two libraries and two museums, and would like to express my appreciation to: Elizabeth Roth and Robert G. Rainwater of the Prints Division, New York Public Library; Sinclair H. Hitchings and R. Eugene Zepp of the Print Department, Boston Public Library; Philip C. F. Smith, Paul Winfisky, Mark Sexton, and Kathy Flynn, Peabody Museum of

Salem; and Elton Hall and Philip Purrington, Old Dartmouth Historical Society Whaling Museum.

Each of the following people has also helped contribute to this book: Nicki Thiras, Addison Gallery of Art; Peter H. Howe, Calendars of Distinction; Vickie Silvis, Museum of Art, Carnegie Institute; D. Roger Howlett and William P. Carl, Childs Gallery; Rowland Elzea, Delaware Art Museum; Forest Fenn, Fenn Galleries; Kenneth R. Martin, Robert Ellis, Kendall Whaling Museum; Gerold M. Wunderlich, F. Frederick Bernaski, Kennedy Galleries; Peter H. Spectre, *The Mariner's Catalog;* John O. Sands, Mariners Museum; Frank Trapp, and his staff, Mead Art Gallery, Amherst; Crosby Forbes, Museum of the American China Trade; Sohei Hohri, New York Yacht Club Library; Paula Matta, Princeton Club of New York Library; George D. Wintress, the Seamen's Bank for Savings; Carlyle Windley, Robert S. Wolk, Seamen's Church Institute of New York; Eleanor Irwin, Union Club Library; D. R. Luke, Venture Prints; William A. Weston, William Weston Gallery, Ltd.

Mark Sexton is responsible for all the photographs from the Peabody Museum, Richard Mason of Creative Photographers for those from the Boston Public Library, David Stansbury for those from the Crossett Collection at Amherst College, and Lewis F. Stockmeyer for those from the Seamen's Church Institute of New York.

Finally, I wish to thank my family and the following people for their encouragement, introductions, ideas, and counsel: Faith Cross, Jay Davis, A. Michael Dowler, Thomas Ettinger, Jr., Nancy Frey, William Guthrie, Cynthia J. Houser, Elizabeth Kennedy, Jeanne Kerr, Noelle King, Eleanor Peters, Don Smith, Celia Sumers, and Julia Weisman.

Glossary

FLEMISH EYE   TURK'S HEAD   CARRICK BEND   BOWLINE   MATTHEW WALKER

"It is very odd that sailor men should talk so queer,"
INGOLDSBY LEGENDS

ABACK: positioned so that sails are pressed against mast by the wind
ABAFT: "aft of," behind
ABEAM: directly off the side of a vessel
AFT, AFTER: toward the stern or back end
AFTER HATCH: cargo hatch nearest the stern
ALL HANDS: the complete crew
ALOFT: above the deck in the rigging
Aloha Oe: Hawaiian, greetings or farewell
AMIDSHIPS: relating to the middle of the vessel
ANCHOR'S AWEIGH: anchor has cleared the bottom
ASTERN: beyond the back end of a vessel; going backward
ASTROLABE: early metal navigation instrument used to determine latitude

BACKSTAYS: standing rigging supporting masts
BAFFLING: frustrating or confusing
BARK, BARQUE: square-rigged sailing vessel with three or more masts, after-mast having fore-and-aft sails only
BEAM ENDS: ends of deck beams
BEAM ENDS, ON HER: canted with deck almost vertical
BEAM SEA: one in which waves run at right angles to a ship's direction
BEAR A HAND: help or assist
BEEVES: plural of "beef"
BELAY: make fast or secure; stop doing
BELAYING PIN: short wood or metal rod used to secure ropes
BERTH: vessel's place in port; sailor's bed
BERTHING: assigning space for a vessel or crew
BIGHT: indentation of a coast; "loop" of a rope
BILGED *(used of a vessel)*: having its bottom punctured
BILGE WATER: water that has seeped into a vessel's bottom
BINNACLE: a protective housing for the compass
BITTS: heavy, short twin posts to hold hawsers
BLOCK: wood or metal shell encasing pulley wheels
BLUE JACKETS: nickname for navy sailors
BLUE PETER: code flag for letter "P," indicates departure
BOARDED: went aboard a vessel
BOARD OF TRADE: British ministry of commerce
BOATSWAIN: petty officer in charge of deck crew

BOATSWAIN'S MATE: assistant to the boatswain
BOGUE: narrow channel of the Pearl River
BOLLARD: short, heavy post used to secure ropes
BOOM: lower spar on a fore-and-aft sail
BOSE: nickname for "boatswain"
BOSUN: phonetic spelling for "boatswain"
BOW: front end of a vessel
BOWLINE: rope to hold forward the weather leech of a square sail; a knot forming a loop
BOWSPRIT: spar projecting beyond the bow
BOWSPRIT'S HEEL: inboard end of a bowsprit
BOW WASH: waves made by vessel's forward motion
BOX: short for "wheelbox"
BRACE(S): rope(s) controlling horizontal motion of yards
BRACE BLOCKS: blocks on the brace tackles
BRACE PINS: special belaying pins used to secure braces
BREACH: to break the water's surface
BREECH: back end of a cannon
BRIG: two-masted, square-rigged vessel
BROACH TO: accidentally swing sideways to the wind
BULKHEADS: inboard "walls" of a vessel
BULWARKS: solid railing along a ship's sides, on the main deck
BUMBOATS: small harbor boats selling supplies
BUNG: stopper used to plug up a cask
BUNT: the middle of a square sail
BUNTING: type of cloth for making flags
BUNTLINES: ropes to help furl a square sail
"BY THE DEEP—NINE": depth of 9 fathoms (54 ft.)
"BY THE MARK—SEVEN": depth of 7 fathoms (42 ft.); lead line marked at 2, 3, 5, 7, 10, 13, 15, 17, 20 fathoms

CABIN BOY: the captain's servant
CABLE: chain or rope attached to the anchor
CABOOSE: small portable cookhouse on deck
CALF: small iceberg broken from a large one
CANTED OVER: heeled or laying toward one side
CANVAS: cotton duck for making sails; the sails themselves
CAPE ST. DIEGO: east end of Tierra del Fuego
CAPE STIFF: seamen's nickname for Cape Horn
CAPSTAN: vertical, barrel-like device to increase pulling power on a rope; see pg. 203
CARAVEL: three-masted vessel with lateen sails
CARRICK BEND: knot joining two ropes
CARRONADE: short-barreled, large-caliber cannon

CARYATIDS: carved stone figures used as support columns
CAUGHT THE CRAB: accidentally caught an oarblade in a wave during stroke recovery
CAY: small, low coral island
CHAIN PLATES: flat bars or rods holding the lower ends of the shrouds to the hull side
CHAINS, CHANNEL: narrow platform on hull side used to spread shrouds
CHAIN-SHEETS: chain controlling a sail's clew
CHANTEY, CHANTY: rhythmic work song
CHART HOUSE: deckhouse used for navigating purposes
CHRONOMETERS: accurate clocks for navigation
CLEW(S): lower corner(s) of a square sail
CLEW UP: take in the clews of a square sail
CLIPPER: a fast-sailing, long, narrow hull, usually ship-rigged
CO-HONG MERCHANTS: shore agents for cargo
COMBER: a large, cresting sea
COMPASS POINT: direction mark on compass card
COURSES: lowest square sails of a vessel
COXSWAIN: helmsman in command of a small boat
CRACK IT (HER) ON: to set excessive sail
CREW: personnel of a vessel
CRINGLE: sort of loop woven into a sail's border rope
CROJICK: phonetic spelling of "crossjack"
CROSSJACK: lowest yard and square sail on the mizzenmast
CROSS-STAFF: early wood navigation instrument
CUMSHAW: a present or gratuity
CUTTER: large, square-sterned rowing boat
CUTWATER: lower edge of a vessel's stem

DAUBER: crew's nickname for a fine-arts painter
DAVIT FALLS: ropes for lowering or raising a boat
DAVY JONES: mythical keeper of sailors' souls
DEADEYE: three-holed wood disk used to set up rigging
DECK: "floor" of a vessel
DECKHOUSES: enclosed structures on the deck
DHOW: Arab vessel with one mast and a lateen sail
DIGHT: poetic, "decked out"
DINGHY: a very small rowing boat
DOCKERS: people who work on piers or docks
DONS: Spanish gentlemen
DOUBLE BANKING: putting two men on each oar
DOUSE THE SAIL: lower or pull it in

DOWNHAULS: ropes for pulling down sails or yards
DOWN HELM: a steering order, to turn a vessel toward the wind

EASE HER: to head temporarily toward wind to reduce stress
EAST INDIAMEN: Far East trading vessels
EIGHT BELLS: 4, 8, and 12 o'clock A.M. & P.M.

FACTORIES: cargo warehouses at Chinese ports
FAIR-LEAD: guide to alter a rope's direction
FALL: the rope of a tackle
FATHOMS: measurements of 6 feet
FIDS: tapered wood spikes for splicing rope
FIFE-RAIL: short pin rail around a mast
FIGUREHEAD: an ornamental carving on the bow
FILLED OUR SHIP AWAY: headed away from the wind
FIVE SEAS OFF: five crest-to-crest wave lengths away
FLEMISH EYE: a type of loop splice in the end of a rope
FLOOD: incoming tide
FLYING JIBBOOM: a spar extending beyond the jibboom
FLYING KITES: setting all light-weather sails
FO'C'SLE: abbreviation of "forecastle"
FO'C'SLEHEAD: raised structure at vessel's bow
FOOTROPE: wire rope below a yard on which men stand
FORE: toward or closest to the bow
FORE-AND-AFT: parallel to the keel
FORECAPSTAN: capstan on a forward deck
FORECASTLE: short superstructure at the bow, the "fo'c'slehead"; also, the seamen's quarters
FOREHATCH: most forward cargo opening in the deck
FORE-HOUSE: most forward deckhouse
FOREMAST: front mast of a sailing vessel
FOREPEAK: triangular space in the lower part of a vessel's bow
FORESAIL: lowest sail on the foremast
FORESAIL FOOT: bottom edge of a foresail
FORE T'GALLANT SAIL: sail above fore topsail
FORE TOPMAST STAYSAIL: triangular headsail
FOREYARD: lowest yard on the foremast
FOULED: opposite of "clear," entangled
FRAP: to bind tightly with ropes
FREEING PORT: opening in the bulwark for water to run overboard
FRESH *(used of winds)*: blowing about 25 m.p.h.
FRESHENING *(used of winds)*: improving or increasing
FRIGATE: ship-rigged war vessel, 24 to 50 guns
FULL AND BY: sailing as close to the wind as possible
FULL FOR STAYS: steer away from the wind for good headway before tacking
FURL: roll up and secure sails
FUTTOCK SHROUDS: iron rods between the top platform and lower mast which take the pull of topmast shrouds

GAFF: spar holding head of a quadrilateral fore-and-aft sail on a mast
GALE: winds from 35 to 56 m.p.h.
GALLEY: the kitchen in a vessel
GALLIOT: small, fast craft with sails and oars
GANTLINE: rope rigged for temporary use
GARTH: archaic for "garden"
GASKET: rope used to secure a furled sail
GATES: doors at entrance of canal locks or basins
GEAR: common term for a vessel's equipment
GELLS: low pronunciation for "girls"
GEORDIE BRIG: slang, a Scottish coasting craft
GIG: captain's special, small-oared boat
GLIM: slang term for a light
GOLDEN NUMBER: the number assigned to a particular calendar year in the Metonic cycle, used in lunar navigation
GONEY: black-footed albatross
GRAMPUS: large member of the dolphin family
GRAPNEL: anchor-like device with hooked arms
GRASSED: scraped
GRATING: latticework platforms or walkways
GREYBEARDS: large, heavy, breaking seas
GROG: mixture, in equal parts, of water and heavy rum
GROGSHOP: sailor's nickname for a saloon
GULLIES: sea gulls, Cape Horn pigeons, and similar birds
GUNNEL: phonetic spelling of "gunwale"
GUN PORTS: cannon openings in a vessel's side
GUNWALE: upper edge of a small boat's side

HALCYON: tranquil and quiet
HALF-DECK: quarters for apprentices and petty officers
HALYARD, HALLIARD: tackle for raising yards, gaffs, and sails; originally "haul yard"
HAND(s): the working seamen of a vessel
HARD A-LEE: put the helm all the way to leeward to turn toward the wind
HARDCASE: slang, a tough person
HARD DOWN YOUR WHEEL: opposite to "hard a-lee" or "down helm"
HARD OVER: bring rudder as far as possible to either side
HATCH, HATCHWAY: an opening in a deck
HAULED HOME: pulled completely into place
HAWSEHOLES: holes in the bow for the anchor cable
HAWSER: large rope for tying up or towing
HEAD: the bow, or front end, of a vessel; the top edge of a sail
HEAD BULWARKS: bulwarks around the bow
HEADSAIL: triangular sail at the bow
HEAVE AND PAWL: push hard on a capstan bar until a pawl drops in a socket
HEAVER: lever bar, a steel spike with wood handle
HEAVING LINE: light rope weighted at one end
HEAVING THE LEAD: finding the depth of water with a lead line
HELM: the tiller, either actual or theoretical
HELMSMAN: the man steering the vessel

HIBERNIAN: an Irishman
HMS: initials for His or Her Majesty's Ship
HOG LANE: disreputable part of Canton
HOLYSTONE: to scour wood decks with sandstones
HOOKER: slang, a vessel
HORNPIPE: lively seaman's dance
HOUSE OF TREE: wooden vessel
HOVE CLEAR: throw or pull free
"HOVE MY SOUL OUT": "I'm exhausted, have given my all"
HOVE TO (used of a vessel): lying head to wind

ISLANDS OF THE BLEST: mythical paradise

JIB: triangular headsail
JIBBOOM: spar extending beyond the bowsprit
JOSS STICKS: slender wands of Chinese incense
JUMPERS: sailors' blouses
JUNK, SALT: pickled beef that has hardened
JUNKS: Chinese seagoing vessels
JURY MAST: makeshift, temporary mast

KANAKA: a native Hawaiian
KEEL: outer backbone of a vessel's structure
KEELSON: inner backbone parallel to the keel
KESTREL: small falcon native to Europe
KETCH: vessel with the shorter of its two masts aft
KITES: light sails of a vessel
KNIGHTHEADS: heavy timbers supporting the bowsprit
KNOCK OFF: stop work
KNOTS: interlacings joining two ropes; speed of a vessel in nautical miles per hour
KREESE: short, wavy-bladed Malayan sword

LADDER: any "stair" in a vessel
LAID THEIR SHIPS ABOARD: came alongside their opponents
LANDFALL: first sighting of land
"LAND HO": lookout's cry upon first seeing land
LANGRIDGE: metal scraps fired from a cannon
LARBOARD: old name for the port side
LASCAR: seaman from the East Indies
LASHING ROPE: rope for tying down things
LAT.: abbreviation for latitude
LATEEN SAIL: triangular sail hung from a sloping yard
LATITUDE(s): angular distance measured north and south from the equator
LAUNCH: large, oared boat for heavy work; to put a boat or vessel into the water
LAY BACK: pull hard on a rope; move backward
LAZARETTE: small storeroom in the stern
LEAD: metal weight on a sounding line
LEADSMAN: man who takes soundings
LEE: the side away from the wind
LEEBOARD: wide board put over the lee side of a shallow-draft sailboat to act as a keel
LEECH: side edge of a square sail
LEE-HELM: when the "tiller" is toward the lee side

LEE-RAIL: rail on the lee side of the vessel
LEEWARD: toward the lee side, pronounced "looard"
LEE-WHEEL: assistant helmsman who stands on lee side
LET DRAW THE HEADSHEETS: slack off jib sheets
LET FLY: loosen and let go suddenly
LET GO AND HAUL: order to swing the foreyards when tacking
LIBERTY: permission to go ashore
LIGHTERS: harbor barges to carry cargo
LINE: the equator
LIST: lean sideways
LOGGERHEAD: small snubbing post in a whaleboat
LOGGING FOURTEEN: going 14 nautical m.p.h.
LOGGING FOURTEEN ON A BOWLINE: as above, with bowlines hauled taut
LON. OR LONG.: abbreviation for longitude
LONG-GLASS BRASS: brass barrel of a telescope
LONGITUDE: angular distance measured east and west from Prime Meridian at Greenwich, England
LOOKOUT: one who keeps watch for approaching objects or events
LOWER TOPSAILS: square sails directly above the courses
LUBBER LINE, LUBBER'S POINT: line on the forward, inner side of a compass bowl representing the bow of the vessel
LUFF: turn a vessel into the wind

MAIN DECK: principal deck of a vessel
MAIN HATCH: primary hatch of a vessel
MAINMAST: second mast of a three-masted craft
MAIN RIGGING: the rigging of the mainmast
MAINSAIL HAUL: order to swing the main and mizzen yards when tacking
MAINSHEET: rope leading aft from each lower corner of the main course
MAIN YARD: lowest yard on the mainmast
MAKE FAST: tie down, secure, belay
MAKE SAIL: unfurl and set the sails
MALL: alternate spelling of maul, a heavy hammer
MARLINE: tarred, two-strand, left-twist hemp cord
MARLINGSPIKE: tapered iron spike used for splicing
MASTHEAD: upper end of mast, above the crosstrees
MASTER: the commander of a merchant vessel
MATE: one of a vessel's officers
MATTHEW WALKER'S ROSES: type of knot
MEET HER WITH THE HELM: counteract the vessel's swing with the rudder
MERIDIAN: imaginary half-circle running from north to south poles
MERSEY: a river at Liverpool, England
MILLS: turns around in the water
MIZZEN CHAINS: slang for mizzen channels
MIZZEN-SHROUDS: standing rigging supporting the mizzenmast

MIZZEN TOPGALLANTS: sails above the topsails
MIZZEN-TOPSAIL: sail above the crossjack
MOLE: stone pier or quay along the shoreline
MOLLIES: "Mollyhawks," birds of Cape Horn
MONSOON: Asiatic winds blowing from SW in summer, NE in winter
MOOR: to anchor; to secure to a pier by ropes
MORGAN, SIR HENRY: Welsh buccaneer (1635–1688)
MULATAS CAYS: NE shoreline of Panama
MUSTER: an assembly of people; to convene or assemble

NAIAD: water nymph
NANTUCKET SLEIGH RIDE: whaleboat being towed by a harpooned whale
NAUTILUS SHELLS: pearly spiral seashells
NIGHT GLASS: low-power telescope for night use
NIPPERMEN: young boys who handled the short ropes (nippers) between the capstan rope and anchor cable
NUKUHEVA: Marquesas Is., South Pacific

Odi et amo: Latin, I hate and I love
OILSKINS: outer garments for wet weather
OLD MAN: nickname for the captain
OLD SALTS: elderly seamen

PAINTER: rope at the bow of a small boat
PALM: sailor's "thimble" for sewing
PANNIKIN: a shallow tin pan
PARACELS: rocky islets in South China Sea
PAYED OFF (used of a vessel): turned away from the wind
PENNON: poetic word for "pennant"
PIER HEAD: the outer end of a pier
PINTLES: pivot pins on which a rudder hangs
PIPE: a series of notes blown on a "bosun's call," a whistle-like instrument
PIPE THE WATCH BELOW: relieve the watch on deck of its duties
PIPING: blowing orders on a bosun's call
PIPING LOUD: blowing hard
PITCH: rock fore and aft, not sideways
POI: Hawaiian food, from the taro root
POINTINGS: fancy tapering of a rope's end
POINTS: one point of the compass is 11¼°; bearings are given in points
POOP: the enclosed space on main deck at stern; to take a sea over the stern
POOP BREAK: front bulkhead of the poop
POOP RAIL: rail around the deck over the poop
POPOCATÉPETL: volcano in Mexico
PORT: left side of vessel when facing forward
PORT MAHONE BABOON: an insulting epithet
PRESS OF CANVAS: large amount of sail set
PRICKERS: pointed instruments used for all canvas work
PROW: the bow, the front end of the vessel
PUNCHEON: large, barrel-like container for wine

QUADRANT: a pre-sextant navigation instrument
QUARTER: side of a vessel near the stern

QUARTERDECK: generally, the after part of the uppermost deck

QUARTER LESS FIVE: a depth less than 5 fathoms

QUIDDING: tobacco-chewing

RAKED: inclined aft from the vertical

RATLINE: foot ropes used to climb rigging

RATTLE DOWN: install ratlines; idiom, to dress up

RED ENSIGN: Great Britain's merchant flag

RED LEAD: rust-resistant paint

REEF: shorten a sail

REEVE CLEAR: assemble a tackle or any running rigging without fouling

RHUMB: constant compass course

RIGGERS: shipyard workers who install rigging

RIGGING: all the ropes and gear of a vessel

RINGBOLT: an eyebolt with a ring inserted

RINGTAIL: light-weather sail extending the spanker

RIO: slang identification of Rio de Janiero

RIO GRANDE: river between U.S. and Mexico

RIVER PLATE: large estuary between Argentina and Uruguay

ROPE YARN: one thread of a strand of rope

ROUSE: to wake or get up

ROYALS: sails above the topgallants

RUNNERS: disreputable recruiters of crews

RUNNING FREE: sailing before the wind

RUNNING GEAR: the moving rigging of a vessel

RUSK: sweet, oven-dried bread; zweiback

SAILS: sailmaker's nickname

SALVING: saving from loss or destruction

SAMPANS: small (10 to 30 ft.) Chinese boats, propelled by sculls or sails

SANTY CRUZ: brand of rum

SCARF: to fit two timbers together

SCHOONER: two-masted vessel with fore-and-aft sails

SCOW: flat-bottomed barge

SCRIMSHANKERS: whalemen who carve articles of whalebone or ivory

SCUDDING: running before a gale with reduced or no sail

SCUPPERS: deck-level drains along a vessel's side

SCUTTLE: deliberately sink a ship

SEA-TOPS: tops of waves

SECOND MATE: officer in charge of a watch

SERVING-MALLETS: tool for winding marline on a rope for protection against weather

SETTEE: a long seat

SHANTY: alternate spelling of "chantey"

SHANTYMAN: lead singer when the crew chanteys on a rope

SHEATHING: planking on the inboard side of bulwarks

SHEAVE: pulley wheel of a block

SHEER: suddenly change course or heading

SHEET: rope controlling the clew of a sail

SHIP: vessel with three or more masts, all square-rigged

SHIP WATER: to have seas wash on board

SHOAL: area of sea bottom close to the water's surface

SHORES: temporary supports holding up a hull

SHROUDS: fixed rigging supporting masts

SHROUD-SCREWS: turnbuckles to tighten rigging

SIDE-SLIP: to move sideways accidentally

SIGNAL FLAGS: flags for transmitting messages

SIGN ON: put one's name on the articles of employment for the voyage

SKYSAILS: sails above the royals

SKYSAIL YARDS: yards above the royal yards

SLAT: flap violently, as sails against masts

SLIP: bed on which a vessel is built

SNORTER: slang, a strong wind

SOUND: to find the depth of water

SOUNDING LINE: a marked line with a lead weight on the end for measuring depths of water in fathoms

SOUTHERN CROSS: four-star constellation in the southern sky

SOU'-WESTER: a type of waterproof hat

SPANISH FOXES: lengths of single, left-twisted yarns

SPANISH WATER: Caribbean and adjacent waters

SPAR: a mast, yard, gaff, or boom

SPINDRIFT: loose spray flying across the sea surface

SPLICE THE MAINBRACE: idiom, to have a drink

SPOKE: communicated by signal flags

SPOKES: radial spindles of a steering wheel

SPUME: foam, frothy water, spindrift

SPURS: short supports under a hull

SPYGLASS: a telescope

SQUALLY: marked by violent gusts of wind with rain

SQUARED AWAY: cleaned up and ready

SQUARE IN THE YARDS: brace the yards crosswise (90° to the keel)

SQUARE-RIGGED: having sails on yards set crosswise on masts

STAMP 'N' GO: push on the bars and turn the capstan around; idiom, to leave

STANCHION: upright post or slender column

STAND BY FOR STAYS: order, prepare to tack a vessel

STAND CLEAR THE CABLE: move away from the anchor cable

STANDING DOWN: boats sailing toward the viewer with wind behind them

STARBOARD: right side of vessel when facing forward

START: first boat to get away

STAYS: fore-and-aft standing rigging

STAYSAILS: triangular fore-and-aft sails

STEADY: hold the vessel's head as ordered

STEERING OAR: extra-long oar for a small boat

STEM: upright structural timber at front end of a hull

STEMSON: inner member of the stem structure

STEP THE MAST: erect the mast

STERN: back end of a vessel

STERN POST: upright timber at back end of a hull, similar to stem

STERNSON KNEE: part of a stern post structure

STIRRUP: short wire rope holding a footrope

ST. LE MARIE: Strait Le Maire, between Tierra del Fuego and Staten Island

St. Mary's: New York school-ship (1874–1907)

STOCKHOLM TAR: viscous fluid distilled from pine roots, used for preserving rope

STOVE IN: broken or holed

STOW: put securely away or store

STRAKE: row of planking or plating on a hull

STROKE: number of pulls per minute; sternmost oarsman

STUDDING SAILS: light sails extending beyond square sails

SWEEPS: extra-large oars for large vessels

SWING PORTS: freeing ports with hinged covers

TACK: change course by turning into the wind

TACKLE: arrangement of two blocks and a fall

TACKLING: collective word for a vessel's ropes

TACKS: ropes leading forward from lower corners of courses

TACKS AND SHEETS: order, to haul up clews of main course and crossjack preparatory to "mains'l haul"

TAFFRAIL: rail at the stern of a hull

TARPAULIN: heavy, tarred, water-repellent canvas

THIMBLE: circular fitting with peripheral groove around which rope is spliced to form an eye

THWARTS: crosswise seats in a small boat

THWART STRINGERS: wood strips on inside of boat to hold thwarts

TILLER: bar on the rudderhead used to turn rudder

TIME BELL: ship's bell

TOGGLES: crosswise wood pins fixed in rope end

TOPGALLANT: situated above the top mast

TOPSAIL: the sail above a course

TOSS OARS: lift oars vertically

TRADE WINDS: almost constant winds from NE and SE between 30° N and 30° S latitudes

TUB: open container of staves, like a half-barrel, for coiled harpoon rope

TURK'S HEAD: a turban-like interweaving of a single rope

TURNING TOP: capsizing

TWENTY-FOUR POUNDER: cannon firing 24-lb. ball

UNDER WAY: a vessel when moving; sometimes, and erroneously, "under weigh"

UNION DOWN: ensign flown upside down, an international distress signal

UNSHIP YOUR BARS: remove the bars from the capstan head

VALERIAN: a plant with white or pink flowers

VANDERDECKEN: the mythical "Flying Dutchman" doomed never to round the Cape of Good Hope

VANG: a rope from the deck to steady a gaff

VEER (*used of the wind*): to change direction to the right

VESSEL: A vessel's a thing on the ocean that floats; the large ones are ships, the small ones are boats

WAIST: middle section of a vessel's main deck

WAKE: the turbulent water astern of a moving vessel

WARE: misspelling of "wear"

WARP: move a vessel about a harbor by pulling on mooring ropes

WASHBOARD: raised, light-wood frame at deck edge

WASHPORTS: see "freeing ports"

WATCH: division of the crew; a duty period

WATERSAIL: light-weather sail set below a spanker boom

WEATHER: being toward the windward side

WEATHER LEECH: windward edge of a square sail

WEATHER ROLL: rocking of a vessel to windward

WHALER: rowboat pointed at both ends

WHAMPOA: anchorage on the Pearl River, China

WHEELBOX: protective housing of the steering gear

WHEEL GRATING: platform on which the helmsman stands

WHEELHOUSE: deck structure surrounding the steering station

WIND FLAW: slight, infrequent breeze

WINDJAMMER: originally a fore-and-aft-rigged sailer, now any sailing vessel

WINDLASS: machine to haul in the anchor cable

WIND'S EYE, INTO THE: directly into the wind

WINDWARD: direction *from* which the wind is blowing

WORE SHIP: changed tack by swinging the stern across the wind

YARD: horizontal spar crosswise on a mast

YARN: a sea story; to tell a story

YAWLS: small, two-masted boats

YOKE LINES: ropes used to steer a small boat

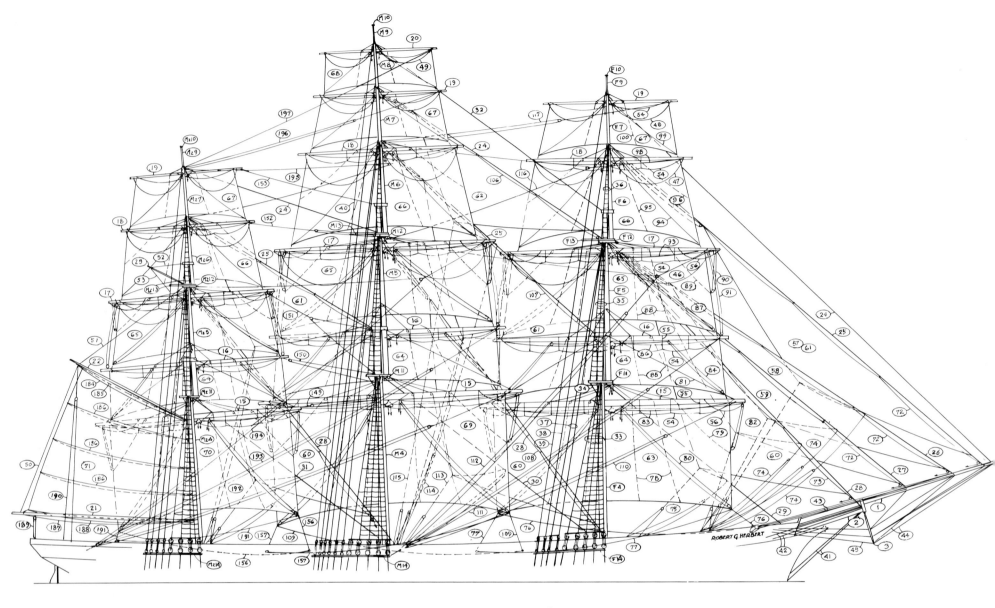

SPAR, RIGGING, AND SAIL PLAN (*Braces shown for one side only*)

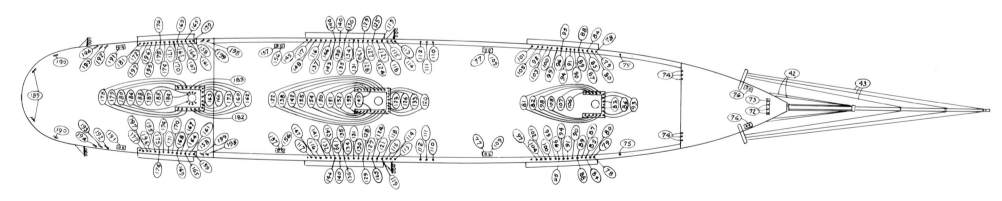

BELAYING PIN PLAN

Nomenclature

SPARS

(F: foremast; M: mainmast; Mz: mizzenmast; e.g., F4 is Fore lowermast. Yards take the name of their mast)

1. Jibboom
2. Bowsprit
3. Martingale boom (dolphin striker)
4. Lowermast
5. Topmast
6. Topgallantmast
7. Royalmast
8. Skysailmast
9. Pole
10. Truck
11. Top
12. Topmast crosstrees
13. Backstay spreaders
14. Channel
15. Lower yard
16. Lower tops'l yard
17. Upper tops'l yard
18. Topgallant yard
19. Royal yard
20. Skys'l yard
21. Spanker boom
22. Spanker gaff
23. Signal, or monkey, gaff

STANDING RIGGING

(Except for the jib stays, takes the name of the mast it supports)

24. Royal stay
25. Topgallant or flying jib stay
26. Outer jib stay
27. Inner jib stay
28. Topmast stay
29. Fore stay
30. Main stay
31. Mizzen stay
32. Skys'lmast stay
33. Lower shrouds
34. Futtock shroud
35. Topmast shrouds
36. Topgallantmast shrouds
37. Topmast backstays
38. Topgallant backstays
39. Royal backstays
40. Skys'lmast backstays
41. Inner and outer bobstays
42. Bowsprit shrouds
43. Jibboom guys

44. Inner and outer martingale stays
45. Backropes
46. Upper tops'l lift
47. Topgallant lift
48. Royal lift
49. Skys'l lift
50. Spanker boom lift
51. Spanker gaff span
52. Signal gaff lift
53. Signal gaff vangs
54. Footrope
55. Stirrup
56. Flemish horse

SAILS

(Square sails take the name of the mast they are on, and staysails take the name of the stay from which they fly)

57. Flying jib, or fore t'gallant stays'l
58. Outer jib
59. Inner jib
60. Topmast stays'l
61. Topgallant stays'l
62. Royal stays'l
63. Fore course or fores'l
64. Lower tops'l
65. Upper tops'l
66. Topgallantsail
67. Royal
68. Skys'l
69. Main course or mains'l
70. Crossjack
71. Spanker

RUNNING RIGGING

(Takes the name of the sail or yard it controls)

72. Flying, outer, and inner jib downhauls
73. Fore topmast stays'l downhaul
74. Flying, outer, and inner jib sheets
75. Fore topmast stays'l sheet
76. Fore tack
77. Fore sheet
78. Fore buntline
79. Fore leechline
80. Fore clewgarnet
81. Fore topping lift
82. Fore reef tackle
83. Fore lower tops'l sheet
84. Fore lower tops'l clewline
85. Fore lower tops'l buntline
86. Fore upper tops'l sheet
87. Fore upper tops'l clewline
88. Fore upper tops'l buntline
89. Fore upper tops'l leechline

90. Fore upper tops'l reef tackle
91. Fore upper tops'l downhaul
92. Fore upper tops'l halyard
93. Fore topgallant sheet
94. Fore topgallant clewline
95. Fore topgallant buntline
96. Fore topgallant leechline
97. Fore topgallant halyard
98. Fore royal sheet
99. Fore royal clewline
100. Fore royal buntline
101. Fore royal halyard
102. Fore topmast stays'l halyard
103. Inner jib halyard
104. Outer jib halyard
105. Flying jib halyard
106. Main royal stays'l downhaul
107. Main topgallant stays'l downhaul
108. Main topmast stays'l downhaul
109. Main tack
110. Fore brace
111. Fore lower tops'l brace
112. Fore upper tops'l brace
113. Main topmast stays'l sheet
114. Main topgallant stays'l sheet
115. Main royal stays'l sheet
116. Fore topgallant brace
117. Fore royal brace
118. Main buntline
119. Main leechline
120. Main topping lift
121. Main clewgarnet
122. Main reef tackle
123. Main lower tops'l sheet
124. Main lower tops'l clewline
125. Main lower tops'l buntline
126. Main upper tops'l sheet
127. Main upper tops'l clewline
128. Main upper tops'l buntline
129. Main upper tops'l leechline
130. Main upper tops'l reef tackle
131. Main upper tops'l downhaul
132. Main upper tops'l halyard
133. Main topgallant sheet
134. Main topgallant clewline
135. Main topgallant buntline
136. Main topgallant leechline
137. Main topgallant halyard
138. Main royal sheet
139. Main royal clewline
140. Main royal buntline
141. Main royal halyard
142. Main skys'l sheet
143. Main skys'l clewline
144. Main skys'l buntline

145. Main skys'l halyard
146. Main topmast stays'l halyard
147. Main topgallant stays'l halyard
148. Main royal stays'l halyard
149. Crossjack brace
150. Mizzen lower tops'l brace
151. Mizzen upper tops'l brace
152. Mizzen topgallant brace
153. Mizzen royal brace
154. Mizzen topgallant stays'l downhaul
155. Mizzen topmast stays'l downhaul
156. Mizzen tack
157. Main sheet
158. Crossjack buntline
159. Crossjack leechline
160. Crossjack topping lift
161. Crossjack clewgarnet
162. Crossjack reef tackle
163. Mizzen lower tops'l sheet
164. Mizzen lower tops'l clewline
165. Mizzen lower tops'l buntline
166. Mizzen upper tops'l sheet
167. Mizzen upper tops'l clewline
168. Mizzen upper tops'l buntline
169. Mizzen upper tops'l leechline
170. Mizzen upper tops'l reef tackle
171. Mizzen upper tops'l downhaul
172. Mizzen upper tops'l halyard
173. Mizzen topgallant sheet
174. Mizzen topgallant clewline
175. Mizzen topgallant buntline
176. Mizzen topgallant leechline
177. Mizzen topgallant halyard
178. Mizzen royal sheet
179. Mizzen royal clewline
180. Mizzen royal buntline
181. Mizzen royal halyard
182. Mizzen topmast stays'l halyard
183. Mizzen topgallant stays'l halyard
184. Spanker head outhaul
185. Spanker head inhaul
186. Spanker brails
187. Spanker clew outhaul
188. Spanker clew inhaul
189. Spanker sheet
190. Spanker vang
191. Mizzen sheet
192. Main brace
193. Main lower tops'l brace
194. Main upper tops'l brace
195. Main topgallant brace
196. Main royal brace
197. Main skys'l brace
198. Mizzen topmast stays'l sheet
199. Mizzen topgallant stays'l sheet

2ᵈ. June. 1923.

TELEPHONE
OYSTER BAY. 357

EFFENDI HILL
OYSTER BAY, LONG ISLAND
NEW YORK

On leaving this hospitable Country where the cream is excellent and the Milk of human Kindness apparently never ceases to flow I assume an ancient mariner's privilege of sending to the Owners and the Ships-Company of the Tusitala my brotherly good wishes for fair winds and clear skies on all their voyages. And may they be many!

And I would recommend to them to watch the weather, to keep the halliards clear for running, to remember that "any fool can carry on but only the wise man knows how to shorten sail in time"... and so on, in the manner of Ancient Mariners of all the world over. But the vital truth of sea-life is to be found in the ancient saying that it is "The stout hearts that make the ship safe".

Having been brought up on it I pass it on to them in all confidence and affection. Joseph Conrad.